AF371511

Focal Points:

Focal Points:

Between a Rock and a Hard Place

Robert Storr

Edited by Francesca Pietropaolo

Heni Publishing, London

Contents

Introduction

by Robert Storr

Lately the U.S. has been undergoing a reckoning with the racial crimes, economic exploitation, and social negligence of its formation. It is not the first such reckoning of this kind. Indeed, the post-Civil War history of the nation—of our deeply Divided States of America—is a tale of what African-American poet and playwright Langston Hughes aptly called "dreams deferred." A tale of the unfinished business of living up to brave promises made to ourselves and to fellow citizens that all too frequently, in fact habitually, have been kicked down the road or slyly left to chance. However, in his seminal poem *Harlem* (1951), Hughes vividly explained the possible outcomes, when he asked and answered the thematic rhetorical question of its opening lines. "What happens to a dream deferred? / Does it dry up / like a raisin in the sun? / Or fester like a sore— / And then run? / Does it stink like rotten meat? / Or crust and sugar over— / like a syrupy sweet? / Maybe it just sags / like a heavy load / Or does it explode?" All of his scenarios have been features of our collective failure to make the most of the chances for social cohesion and social justice that our ancestors nominally fought for during the American Revolution, along with every war since, and that we pretend to celebrate on the 4th of July.

My entire life has been lived in the long shadow cast by this tragic, potentially catastrophic default, a shadow seemingly quickened by periodic spasms of outrage and violence. Obvious open wounds and profound, always palpable, internalized hurt are the proof of our plight. Cognizance or denial of that painful reality are, for better but mostly for worse, what defines us as individuals but also as a country. The essay "Between a Rock and a Hard Place" featured in this book was originally commissioned by Archibald Gillies, who created The Andy Warhol Foundation for the Visual Arts based on a wish expressed by the artist in a handwritten note following his untimely death in 1987.[1] Among the Foundation's first initiatives was a series of papers on art, culture, and society written by critics and historians. Lest casual readers jump to the conclusion that political and social concerns were far from Warhol's mind, one has only to look at his depictions of race riots, the funeral of JFK, and war to realize that quite the opposite was true. Death and destruction and their causes suffuse his work with the stench of sweat, blood, and broken, charred bodies. That Warhol coded or disguised his outlook and convictions goes hand in glove with his position as a contemporary "dandy" and a gay man navigating a "straight" world. Accordingly, many of the drag queens he obsessively pursued with his camera, like the wunderkind with whom he became infatuated in the final years of his life, were African American. Nevertheless, that recognition insistently points to his habit of "queering" anything and everything he laid his eyes on or set his hand to. It also bears mentioning that Warhol's scope encompassed the works of the German Marxist playwright and poet Bertolt Brecht whom he cites in his wonderfully caustic and mercurial book *The Philosophy of Andy Warhol (From A to B and Back Again)* (1975), while declaring his desire to accomplish what Brecht aimed to do but without Communism.

As I stated early on in the "Between a Rock and A Hard Place" essay, "For the better part of my life I have lived hard by the color line." My choice of words was very deliberate then—I meant better qualitatively, not just quantitatively—and they echo prophetically now that I have traveled through regions of uniform financial security and entitlement, as well as monochrome enclaves of "whiteness" previously unknown to me thanks—or no thanks—to jobs in the Ivy League and at major museums, which were wholly beyond my ken when setting out. So permit me to fill in a few blanks in my "resumé" as sketched in what follows.

1 Editor's note: Archibald Gillies was the president of The Andy
   Warhol Foundation for the Visual Arts from 1990 to 2001.

My father hailed from Fort Wayne, Indiana and Olivet, Michigan, and my mother from Evanston, Illinois and Benton Harbor, Michigan. Both attended Swarthmore College, outside Philadelphia, Pennsylvania, as, eventually, did I. My father came from straitened middle-class circumstances following the early death of his father and brother, and a depressing life with a mother who opened a rooming house to support them. My mother issued from more prosperous ones, which she was at pains not to take for granted. Both went to graduate school in Cambridge, Massachusetts, she at Radcliffe College, where she studied history under the distinguished but unapologetically sexist Samuel Eliot Morison, he at Harvard University where he wrote his dissertation on the foundations of higher education in the U.S.—an unsexy topic for the period—under Arthur M. Schlesinger Sr.[2] After volunteering for service in the Army Airforce, my father spent the traumatizing duration of the conflict island hopping in the Pacific theater, and found his first postwar job—which paid something in the vicinity of $2,500 annually—at Bowdoin College in Brunswick, Maine. His second posting was at Howard University in Washington, D.C. where he was invited to replace his Harvard classmate and fellow Schlesinger student John Hope Franklin—who came from Tulsa, Oklahoma where his lawyer father was the go-to counsel for the African-American victims of the 1921 Tulsa Race Massacre, one of the worst episodes of racial violence in our history.[3] My father and Franklin remained in touch for the remainder of their lives, though their perspectives diverged increasingly after 1968. One day, when I worked as curator at The Museum of Modern Art in New York, I heard Franklin calling

2 Editor's note: Arthur M. Schlesinger Sr. (1888–1965), American historian whose emphasis on social and urban developments greatly broadened approaches to U.S. history.

3 Editor's note: John Hope Franklin (1915–2009), African-American historian specializing in Southern and African-American history. He wrote the seminal book *From Slavery to Freedom* (1947). In the course of his career, Franklin had professorships at St. Augustine College, North Carolina College, Howard University, Brooklyn College, University of Chicago, and Duke University.

out to me on the street after visiting the museum. I still vividly remember a Henry Ossawa Tanner that hung in his house, down the block from ours, in Hyde Park in Chicago.[4] I recall that my father, returning Franklin's kindness at Howard, had helped to bring him to teach at the University of Chicago.

The Sixties were years of tension, dispute, and occasional violence in our ethnically "marbled" neighborhood, an island of conservative academic power in the strife-riven predominantly Black South Side of Chicago. My vantage point as a "faculty brat" was enhanced by the job I had selling newspapers and books at a local shop where, along with those who otherwise lived in the neighborhood, I met many figures of note who were just passing through. Among those pertinent to this essay were the African-American historian Lerone Bennett, Jr., author of *Before the Mayflower* (1962) and of the demystifying *Forced into Glory: Abraham Lincoln's White Dream* (2000); the American economic historian and social scientist Robert William Fogel, a former Marxist turned Neo-Con—a commonplace about-face post 1968—whose revisionist study of the economics of slavery, *Time on the Cross*, provoked an uproar when it came out in 1974; the African-American playwright, director, and actor Douglas Turner Ward, founder of the Negro Ensemble Company and a friend of "Bob" Fogel (who was Jewish and White) and his wife Enid (who was Black). Their son, Michael, who lived across the street from me, was one of my best buddies in middle school and high school. Then there were the African-American writer Gwendolyn Brooks—who I heard read in a local auditorium—and the boxer and activist Muhammad Ali, whose main mosque was just beyond Hyde Park, and whose girlfriend of those years, Portia, lived within the neighborhood. Hearing Ali explain to a nearly empty field

4 Editor's note: Henry Ossawa Tanner (1859–1937), African-American artist. He earned international acclaim largely through his religious paintings. In 1923 the French government made him a Chevalier of the Legion of Honor, and in 1927 he became the first African American to be granted full membership in the National Academy of Design in New York.

house at the university why he, who had filled stadiums, wouldn't go to Vietnam had an enormous impact on my nearing-draft-age, Quaker-leaning mind. Finally, there was the African-American singer, poet, and playwright Oscar Brown, Jr. who, with his wife Jean Pace, produced a consciousness-raising musical review in a church pastored by the father of a high-school classmate of mine. Reverend Fry had reached out to local warring gangs—the Blackstone Rangers and the Disciples—and attempted to arrange for a truce between them and a surrender of their weapons. Brown's show in the nave of the sanctuary was a test of Fry's influence over the Blackstone Rangers, which, with little if any change in their criminal operations, became notorious after a full-on relapse into gangsterism, first as the Almighty Black P. Stone Nation, then as El Rukn.

In sum, I did not learn about racial "difference" much less "intersectionality" in a seminar room, though it is better to learn from books and teachers than not at all. Rather, I learned about racial issues from daily contacts and frictions, or what used to be known as "the school of hard knocks." On that score, I have left out numerous muggings, and other more jarring forms of exposure to American racism Black-on-White, White-on-Black. So if my face and body remain unscarred after twenty-plus years of close calls (including having my neck cut during a robbery in Boston by a knife-wielding kid more scared by his aggression than I), my psyche is not. All of that came with me to our "hood" in Flatbush, Brooklyn, where I lived in the late 1980s and early 1990s with my wife and two daughters, and to work at MoMA in midtown Manhattan. Along with a powerful longing to somehow resolve the double consciousness—in due deference to W. E. B. Du Bois who originated that concept—that I brought to the edge of the abyss between the races. More than anything, this schizophrenic "identity" as a "stone" WASP with what seemed on paper to be the full pedigree, but also with a wealth—here again I choose my words advisedly—of experience falling a long way from the norm for a man of my outward appearance, publicly known background, and professional role is what I brought to my unplanned, unforeseen, and thoroughly unconventional "life in art."

What I found at MoMA in 1990 was a hot mess masquerading as cool sovereignty over divisions that were as obvious to outsiders as they were under wraps for in-house protagonists. One such outsider was Akosua Barthwell Evans, a Yale-educated attorney and business woman, who had created an Afrocentric support group at the Detroit Institute of Arts, and launched a similar initiative at MoMA in 1993, three years after my arrival at the museum. The latter group became known, euphemistically, as the Friends of Education because the senior administration of the museum was uncomfortable sponsoring an overtly ethnic organization within its midst. With its most sophisticated members being the Newport Jazz Festival impresario George Wein and his African-American wife, Joyce, Agnes Gund, and David Rockefeller, Jr., beyond them it encompassed a fairly wide range of ages and experience but in the main was esthetically conservative. Such that when I, as its first staff adviser, asked for support from the Friends to help with the acquisition of a black monochrome painting by Glenn Ligon, they demurred. Conversely, a white member who had initially agreed to acquire a sculpture by Elizabeth Catlett got cold feet and backed out. On both sides of the esthetic dividing line between "traditional" figuration and "progressive" abstraction, patrons seemed to fear being caught out when decisions were finally made, and squeamish insecurity ruled, such that the paucity of acquisitions that may have read as subliminal "racism" was often the result of established "taste" in different camps. From beyond the grave, the American critic Clement Greenberg continued to tip the scale as he had done through the reign of MoMA Chief Curator William Rubin from 1968 to 1988. It was Rubin's capriciously exclusive version of "modernism" that gave MoMA its reputation for conservatism and cultural bias, not the model of a modern museum created and

overseen by its founder Alfred H. Barr, Jr. for most of its history
from 1929 to 1968.

After all, Barr's museum had welcomed folk sculptor William
Edmondson, heroic social realist Elizabeth Catlett (incidentally
the first wife of painter, printmaker, and muralist Charles White),
and Norman Lewis whom Barr invited to join the pivotal panel that
he moderated in 1950 at Studio 35 in New York at which the basic
tenets of New York School art were propounded and debated by the
likes of William Baziotes, Louise Bourgeois, Willem de Kooning,
Robert Motherwell, and Ad Reinhardt. Arguably Barr's most
important addition to MoMA's art by black artists was half of Jacob
Lawrence's epic *The Migration Series* (1940–41), the other half of
which went to the Phillips Collection in Washington, D.C. (A series
of sixty paintings, this seminal work dramatically depicts the Great
Migration, the mass movement of African Americans from the
rural South to the urban North.)

Furthermore, at MoMA was active the Trinidadian-born curator
Kynaston McShine who worked in various curatorial capacities
there (from Exhibition Assistant to Chief Curator at Large) from
1959 to 2008—with, in between, a shorter experience working at
the Jewish Museum in New York (from 1965 to 1967 as Curator of
Painting and Sculpture; and from 1965 to 1968 as Acting Director),
where he mounted two of his most adventurous and influential
exhibitions, *Primary Structures* (1966) and *Yves Klein* (1967). At
MoMA, McShine organized the seminal exhibition *Information*
(1970) on international Conceptual art practices, and monographic
presentations of artists such as Joseph Cornell, Marcel Duchamp, Andy
Warhol, and Richard Serra, as well as the exhibition *The Museum as
Muse* (a 1999 stab at insider institutional critique), among others.
And yet, during his entire period at the museum, McShine was the
only African-diasporic person holding full curatorial rank at MoMA.

By 2019, in the context of the profound changes called for in
culture and society by the Black Lives Matter movement, the balance

began to shift decisively toward an openness to true diversity and the collections started to reflect that fact. The appointments of A. C. Hudgins and Anna Deavere Smith to MoMA's board of trustees were both signs of the recognition that Black Lives Mattered and Black Art too. And, that they mattered to the entire enterprise of accounting for "modern," if not "modernist," art in the present as well as the past. In 2014 MoMA brought in the African-American scholar Darby English—who would work there as Adjunct Curator through 2020—to take inventory of the collections and publish a catalogue of their African and Afro-diasporic components. That massive volume, *Among Others: Blackness at MoMA* (2019), co-edited by English and Charlotte Barat, is an impressive publication! A document that is only flawed insofar as it doesn't fully track the periods of activity in this field, or account for all the players. Nevertheless, it is a milestone, which can be added on to and deepened whenever MoMA wishes—or feels pressure to do so.

Alfred H. Barr, Jr. comes first historically because of his wide-ranging view of what modern art could be and his own entrepreneurship in this domain, including not only the acquisition of works by stone carver Edmondson, drawings by Lewis, and paintings by Horace Pippin, but also works by Haitian "folk artists" such as Philomé Obin, among other early examples. Over the decades, more prints by Catlett, collages by Romare Bearden and Howardena Pindell (the latter a MoMA staffer in various capacities for a dozen years), sculptures by Mel Edwards and Richard Hunt (who was given a solo show in 1971 at the museum), canvases by William T. Williams and Sam Gilliam, as well as photographs by Roy DeCarava, James Van Der Zee, and Dawoud Bey entered MoMA's canon. And yet, they have all too frequently languished in storage thereafter. During my tenure at MoMA as curator and subsequently senior curator (1990–2002), I attempted but failed to bring in major works by Catlett, Alison Saar, and Adrian Piper. However, I was successful with my first ever acquisition, that of *High Falutin'* (1990) by David Hammons who, with Piper, was in my first major MoMA exhibition *DIS*LOCATIONS. Incidentally, her installation *What It's Like, What It Is #3* (1991) entered MoMA's holdings many years after I commissioned it for my inaugural show.[5] Other acquisitions that I was able to see through during my time at the museum were the first Norman Lewis paintings to enter MoMA's collection, *Phantasy II* (1946) and *Untitled* (1949), both gifts of the Friends of Education in 1998. Moreover, I ushered in Ellen Gallagher's collage on canvas *Oh! Susanna* (1995), Glenn Ligon's *White #19* (1994), photographs by Seydou Keïta—one, *Untitled (Bamako)* (1949–52), was my gift in honor of Sally Ganz— plus *Condemnation Without Trial* (1989–90) by Chéri Samba, and *Emergency Room* (1989) by Robert Colescott—the latter was acquired in collaboration with my colleague Carolyn Lanchner. Meanwhile, other contributions to the collection were made at the behest of patrons with their own connections to art and artists, in which case I was more a facilitator than an initiator. Thus, I played a role in bringing the drawings of "outsider" Minnie Evans to MoMA. Agnes Gund and her husband Daniel Shapiro prompted the acquisition of sculptures by the Senegalese artist Moustapha Dimé and the African Americans Terry Adkins (a former studio art faculty colleague at the University of Pennsylvania) and Martin Puryear (about whom I had written an essay for his entry in the São Paulo Biennial of 1989, at which he was awarded the grand prize).[6]

This admittedly long, detailed, and zig-zagging introduction is not intended to be in any sense a complete account of what went on at MoMA while I was on staff, nor provide the full picture of what preceded or followed my time there. Neither do I wish to claim credit for more than my share of "wins" in this heavily contested area. My

5 Editor's note: Adrian Piper's *What It's Like, What It Is #3* (1991) entered MoMA's collection in 2017.

6 Editor's note: the essay on Martin Puryear referred to is Robert Storr, "Martin Puryear: The Hand's Proportion," in Kellie Jones and Robert Storr, *Martin Puryear: 20a Bienal Internacional de São Paulo 1989*, exh. cat. (Jamaica Arts Center, Jamaica, N.Y., 1989), pp. 25–34.

concern is the presence or absence of crucial pieces to the puzzle of modern art, not who put them in play, since the reassembling of them will continue for generations to come and that process will fundamentally alter, as well as, in the aggregate, enhance, our appreciation of what modern art has consisted of and meant since Tahitian sculpture provided Paul Gauguin with formal templates for his "exotic" reveries, and "appropriated" African tribal art kicked off Cubism. However, I did want to show what my stake in diversifying the museum was, what I did because of my sense of responsibility as one of the gatekeepers of one of the bellwether museums in the world. I trust that this preamble dovetails with and will shed useful light on the essay "Between a Rock and a Hard Place," which is the primary focus of this book.

While much has been achieved since the mid-1990s, when I wrote "Between a Rock and a Hard Place," a lot still needs to be done to continue to diversify museums' collections and their audiences, as well as the curatorial and management staff leading our institutions. The urgency is palpable and the call for change is profoundly felt especially by the young generations, many of whom work in those institutions and feel the contradictions upon which my essay centers even more acutely than I. We need to come together. More than ever, we should be mindful of Gwendolyn Brooks's poetic words (originally dedicated to Paul Robeson): "We are each other's harvest: / we are each other's / business: / we are each other's / magnitude and bond."

Hope Is the Thing with Feathers
That Perches in the Soul

by Francesca Pietropaolo

This book grapples with one of the most critical topics at the heart of American culture and society, that is, the racial divide and issues of identity and representation, as explored in what is, arguably, one of Robert Storr's most "personal" essays—here the personal intertwines with the political, in the broad sense of the latter term—"Between a Rock and a Hard Place." This piece, a lesser-known one among his writings, was first published in 1994 by The Andy Warhol Foundation for the Visual Arts, which commissioned it for its *Paper Series on the Arts, Culture, and Society*.[1] Featured here in a revised edition, it is made available to a broader public—as part of the new *Focal Points* series gathering selected monographic writings by Storr on a single artist or theme—and, in particular, to a young generation tackling with renewed urgency these fundamental issues in contemporary life and society where, following the Black Lives Matter movement begun in 2013, groundbreaking changes have started to emerge.

While rooted in the context of the 1990s, which witnessed the ascendance of multiculturalism and a heated debate around it—a complex historical juncture that Storr contributes to unravel— "Between a Rock and a Hard Place," read today, thirty years after its writing, voices questions, tensions, concerns, and aspirations that resonate with the current cultural debate.

1 For an overview of Storr's criticism from its beginnings to the present, see the two-volume collection Robert Storr, *Writings on Art 1980–2005*, Francesca Pietropaolo ed. (Heni, London, 2020) and Robert Storr, *Writings on Art 2006–2021*, Francesca Pietropaolo ed. (Heni, London, 2021).

As a further reading relating to the critical subject of the present *Focal Points: Between a Rock and a Hard Place* volume, see Storr's conversations with the artists Wangechi Mutu, Jack Whitten, and Kara Walker respectively, where, among other topics, issues of race and identity are tackled, in the anthology Robert Storr, *Interviews on Art*, Francesca Pietropaolo ed. (Heni, London, 2017), pp.557–567 (Mutu's interview); pp.857–865 (Walker's interview); pp.877–911 (Whitten's interview).

In his essay, Storr tackles the challenging issues of race and diversity from the vantage point of his experience as a member of the art community: specifically, as a white man living in a richly diverse neighborhood in Brooklyn, Flatbush (that is, what was then considered periphery), of which he vividly describes the moments of coming together as well as the racial and social tensions; and as a curator in the then predominantly white and male world of one of the most influential centers of the American art world and one of the most important modern art museums in the world, New York's Museum of Modern Art.[2] As Storr writes in the introductory part of his text: "The tension between the world in which I lived ... and that in which I worked ... motivated me to write and informs all aspects of what follows." As he further articulates in the course of his essay, "Affirming black identity in the face of white indifference or hostility is not just the affair of activists, and certainly not the conceit of social theorists, but a daily struggle for collective recognition, reconciliation, and survival in which everyone is engaged without choice or exception."

Focusing on the New York art scene—as a critic and curator, he was establishing himself as an important voice in it as well as internationally—Storr reflects on the meaning and value of cultural diversity in the U.S., as well as on the role of modern art museums and multiculturalism in art. Incidentally, his growing up for the most part in Chicago's predominantly Black South Side section, which Storr recalls in his introduction to this volume, can be regarded as a formative aspect that has had important

2   Meaningfully, Storr has recalled that, when invited to work at MoMA by the late Kirk Varnedoe, he reached out to Felix Gonzalez-Torres for advice: "... I asked some friends and the friend who made the difference was Felix Gonzalez-Torres. I asked Felix, 'What happens if I do this? Will I be completely cut off from my community? Will it mean that I joined the establishment and I will become a pariah?' And he responded, 'No, no, it will be really great to have one of us inside.' ... When I moved from being a free-agent critic and curator to being a temporary museum man I saw it as a larger field of activity. A place for on-the-job, on-site 'institutional critique'." See "Interviewing Is a Form for Finding Out: Conversation with Francesca Pietropaolo," in Robert Storr, *Interviews on Art*, Francesca Pietropaolo ed. (Heni, London, 2017), pp.22–23.

reverberations in the development of his sustained involvement in the art of African-American and African artists.

Storr explores MoMA's history, pointing at aspects of the museum's exhibition and acquisition programming that reflected MoMA's founding director Alfred H. Barr, Jr.'s far-reaching vision and his involvement in a plurality of art forms and cultures. (Visual glimpses into MoMA's early exhibition history are given through several installation views reproduced in this volume's plate section, comprising also images of selected artworks discussed in it and photographic portraits of poets invoked in Storr's essay such as Gwendolyn Brooks, Allen Ginsberg, Langston Hughes, and Walt Whitman.) Overall, Storr reflects on the strengths and flaws in MoMA's history in relation to multiculturalism and, in his introduction to this book, looking back on his "Between a Rock and a Hard Place" piece, he enriches the topic with telling examples culled from the history of the museum during his tenure there (1990–2002), and beyond.[3]

Since the 2010s onward, notably in response to the call for social and cultural change initiated by the Black Lives Matter movement in the U.S., which reverberated globally, MoMA has made great advancements in diversifying its collection and exhibitions. (Parallel to that, since the 2010s things have profoundly improved also in terms of the diversification of its curatorial voices, finally changing a situation where, still in the 2000s—when I worked at the museum—only two curators of color were on the museum staff: the then Chief Curator at Large Kynaston McShine and the then curatorial assistant, in the Painting and Sculpture Department and afterwards in the Department of Photography, Sarah E. Lewis, currently an acclaimed writer and influential associate professor of history of art and architecture and African and African American studies at Harvard University.)

---

3 For further reading, see *Among Others: Blackness at MoMA*, Darby English and Charlotte Barat eds. (The Museum of Modern Art, New York, 2019), a first assessment of the institution's legacy in displaying, acquiring, and otherwise engaging work by Black artists.

Consider as a case in point the representation of Sondra Perry (b.1986) in MoMA's holdings. In 2017 five works by her, all made just the previous year, entered the museum's collection, followed in 2022 by the acquisition of a seminal 2013 work, the two-channel, high-definition silent video *Double Quadruple Etcetera Etcetera I & II*, which masterfully explores issues of historically erased bodies as well as "slippages of identity" in the current digital world. Calling to mind the works *Cornered* (1988) and *Out of the Corner* (1990) by Adrian Piper, in which, like in Perry's piece, the experience of being in a corner—or better said, *cornered*—is a central symbolic element, Perry's work captures in each of the two videos a performer frenetically dancing in the corner of a white room. In each video, the body is rendered nearly invisible by way of a computer function, which ceaselessly attempts to fill it with the white wall behind it. Only the performer's hair—a marker of racial identity—is unaffected by the software and defies erasure. In 2023 this work was included in MoMA's collection-based exhibition *Signals: How Video Transformed the World* (organized by Stuart Comer and Michelle Kuo).

Providing a from-the-field report taking the pulse of the situation as it unfolded, "Between a Rock and a Hard Place" addresses examples of innovative contemporary art dealing with the complexities of identity representation, notably featured for the first time in two museum exhibitions, respectively *DIS*LOCATIONS (1991–92), Storr's own inaugural project at MoMA since his appointment as curator in 1990, and the 1993 Whitney Biennial organized by curators Thelma Golden, John G. Hanhardt, Lisa Phillips, and Elisabeth Sussman at the Whitney Museum of American Art. Aiming to introduce provocative contemporary practices in the "House of Modernity," in *DIS*LOCATIONS Storr presented installation works made for the exhibition by a diverse range of artists: Louise Bourgeois, Chris Burden, Sophie Calle, David Hammons, Ilya Kabakov, Bruce Nauman, and Adrian Piper.

In these pages, Storr recalls, "I arrived at MoMA at just the moment when the old dogmas were imploding under pressure from critical theory, while being exploded by eclectic contemporary artistic practices that they could neither explain, accommodate, nor constrain." *What It's Like, What It Is #3* (1991; **plate 17**) by Piper and *Public Enemy* (1991; **plates 18** and **19**) by Hammons, the latter no longer extant, are the works on which Storr insightfully focuses here.

The 1993 Whitney Biennial, which aimed at pushing the boundaries of the very definition of American art to include a plurality of voices until then largely overlooked, with an emphasis on works confronting issues of race, gender, and sexuality, provoked a backlash and an extremely heated debate at the time. Moreover, in relation to the context of those years, it is important to underline that the climate of the early 1990s was marked by deep racial tensions in the U.S. In this connection, tellingly the 1993 Whitney Biennial chose to include an amateur video that recorded the brutal police beating of a young African American, Rodney King, which had sparked the Los Angeles riots of 1992.

Rather than reviewing the Whitney exhibition to discuss its overall curatorial outcome, Storr intentionally focuses on some of the works that it brought to public attention, which are relevant to the topic he tackles in his essay: in particular, *Notes on the Margin of the Black Book* (1991–93; **plates 30** and **31**) by Glenn Ligon and *Synecdoche* (1991–92; **plate 29**) by Byron Kim.

In "Between a Rock and a Hard Place," the critic points at the richness of Black art underscoring the great accomplishments of artists of different generations. He celebrates, in particular, the rise in the 1990s of a young generation of African-American artists contributing to an "artistic flowering that more than rivals the 'Harlem Renaissance' of the 1920s and 1930s in its vigor, range of expression, and accomplishment." Among them are Dawoud Bey, Gary Simmons, Lorna Simpson, Kara Walker, Carrie Mae Weems, and Fred Wilson, to name just a few—that is, some of American art's most influential voices of our time.

With its historically, geographically, and culturally specific perspective and its ability to reach beyond that, "Between a Rock and a Hard Place" constitutes today a relevant source helping us to think about the complexities of issues of race and representation in the continuing process of raising awareness and building agency, one where historical memory is as crucial as the power of imagination in order to *make* the future. A recent milestone in such a process, achieved in the effort to expand globally the knowledge and representation of the architecture, art, and culture of Africa and the African diaspora, and to challenge and transform the current power structure, is the 2023 Venice Biennale of Architecture for which its artistic director, the Ghanaian-Scottish Lesley Lokko, organized the exhibition *The Laboratory of the Future*. My experience of it, which took place as I set out to write the present introduction in May 2023, was filled with thought-provoking discoveries. In the brief discussion of Lokko's undertaking that follows—as a coda to this introduction—the aim is to bridge what is for current readers the *historical* perspective offered by Storr's essay and the contemporary situation—the *then* and the *now*, inextricably linked.

In Lokko's Venice Biennale, within its signature international framework, African and African-diasporic current creative output took center stage, contributing to the exploration of a richly expanded notion of architecture that celebrates interdisciplinarity. The exhibition also included an inspiring documentary film on the Black Artists Retreat, an annual gathering of Black artists across disciplines and from all over the world initiated in 2013 by the Chicago-based artist Theaster Gates. This film, realized by Gates to mark the convening's ten-year existence and shown for the first time in *The Laboratory of the Future*, captures the creation of a "temporary social architecture" through the experience of gathering. Notably, in it we see established artists—such as Dawoud Bey, Carrie Mae Weems, and Deborah Willis, among others—engage in discussions with a younger generation of practitioners.[4]

To borrow Emily Dickinson's poetic words, "'Hope' is the thing with feathers— / that perches in the soul—."[5] As we struggle for the representation and embrace of diversity in human society across the spectrum and for a new relationship with the natural and built environment, in the hope for a better future, Lokko's endeavor is groundbreaking. In her show, contemporary African and African-diasporic creativity not only gains full visibility but, in a step further, affords fundamental sources for inspiration in the complex process of rethinking how to address some of the most pressing issues for humanity today.

Suggesting that the "future is ancestral," and that active memory and mind-bending creativity, combined, are key to advance our vision, *The Laboratory of the Future* invited us to come together and explore transformative ways to create our future. Upon entering the Biennale exhibition at the Arsenale, one encountered a space suspended in the tenuous reverberation of blue light—referencing the blue hour, just before sunrise or just after sunset—the light of renewal where changes are suggested as possible in a mixture of elation for the new and a subtle melancholy for what inevitably we need to leave behind of ourselves in the process of transformation. Left empty to house a nuanced installation of light, mirroring surfaces and text-based projections on the walls, that inaugural room powerfully encapsulated the experience of *being in* space and *making* space, as we inhabited it momentarily both physically and with our imagination. It evoked the moment of a new beginning as, reflected in the slightly warped

4 The film is *Black Artists Retreat (B.A.R.): Reflections on 10 Years of Convening* (2023).

5 From Emily Dickinson's poem *"Hope" is the thing with feathers* from c. 1861 whose first stanza reads: "'Hope' is the thing with feathers— / that perches in the soul— / and sings the tunes without the words / —and never stops—at all—." The title of this introductory text is a quote from it.

mirrors together with other visitors, we recognized ourselves as agents in the creation of new multiple spaces. By using the craft of exhibition-making as tool, in this and other instances, Lokko invited us to unlearn systems of knowledge to begin imagining unprecedented possibilities.

Among the words projected on the walls on each side of the room were the following ones by James Baldwin that stayed with me and whose powerful reflection deeply resonate with the complex subject of this book, as well as with the urgent desire, at the current historical juncture, to find new ways to make the future:

> *The world changes according to the way people see it, and if you alter, even by a millimeter, the way … people look at reality, then you can change it.*[6]

6 James Baldwin, interview by Mel Watkins, *New York Times Book Review*, 23 September 1979, p.37.

Between a Rock
and a Hard Place

This is the revised version of the essay first published as Robert Storr, Between a Rock and a Hard Place *(The Andy Warhol Foundation for the Visual Arts, New York, 1994).*

Introductory Note

The meaning and value of cultural diversity in America are not topics
open to purely objective or theoretical assessment. Nobody enjoys
a truly global view and no one can claim to speak from a totally
disinterested vantage point. Whites, in particular, must be careful
to avoid any such pretense, since in too many cases it means that
they are passing judgment on the personal testimony of non-whites
without accounting for their own experience or clearly establishing
their everyday perspective on the social realities involved. This
essay on the role of modern art museums and multiculturalism
was, therefore, conceived in two parts. The first speaks briefly but
I hope usefully about the situation in which I found myself when
the issue came to a head for me professionally. The second deals
both first-hand and historically with the esthetic, political, and
practical problems entailed in addressing the fact of pluralism in
art. The tension between the world in which I lived, as represented
in part one, and that in which I worked, as represented in part two,
motivated me to write and informs all aspects of what follows.

Part I

Always a knit of identity ... always distinction ... always a breed of life.
— Walt Whitman[1]

For the better half of my life, I have lived hard by the color line. For
the last seven years, I lived on the other side. The neighborhood was
Flatbush, Brooklyn; my neighbors were, for the most part, African
American and West Indian. Situated on the "far edge" of Prospect
Park, the section of Flatbush in which I settled is a mix of large, old
apartment buildings, small stores with living quarters above, and

1 Walt Whitman, *Leaves of Grass*, first ed. 1855
  (Viking Press, New York, 1961), p.27.

ornate brownstones. The brownstones have remained undivided and intact thanks to the covenant imposed by the farmer who deeded his land to developers at the turn of the century with the stipulation that the houses built on it were to remain single-family dwellings in perpetuity. Over the many economic cycles since, and the transition from generation to generation and from one ethnic group to another, this pact, closely observed, has kept slumlords and gentrifying speculators away from the tree-lined and well-tended residential blocks that branch off Flatbush Avenue.

Traffic on that main artery is heavy, and the action on the corners is often "heavy" as well. Chinese and Caribbean restaurants and Hispanic *bodegas* occupy most of the intersections between the avenue and the side streets; drug runners command the pay phones planted by the curb. Despite this human flux, and the fear of violence that shadows the street's vital commotion, the shopkeepers, executives, office workers, teachers, lawyers, artisans, householders, short- and long-term unemployed, pensioners, and children who populate the neighborhood all recognize one another, and know that they are known, even to those who look away as they pass.

Surrounded by the teeming vastness of the city, the district is a distinct but far from homogeneous world. On the map, its cardinal compass points are the Park, the Botanic Garden, the Brooklyn Museum, Kings County Hospital, and Ebbets Field—former home to the Brooklyn Dodgers and now a massive public housing project. Legend has it that when Jackie Robinson signed up with the team in the late 1940s, he tried to buy a house in the area so he could walk to work, but couldn't find a seller.[2] A few years later, the once all-white section was nearly all black. It stayed middle- and working class. Other landmarks include the grocery store on Church Avenue,

2 Editor's note: Jack Roosevelt Robinson (1919–1972), American baseball player and the first African American to play in Major League Baseball in the modern era, when he joined the Brooklyn Dodgers in 1947. (The Major Leagues had not had an African-American player since 1889, when baseball became segregated.)

which in 1990 was the target of a months-long boycott by community members and activists who accused the Korean immigrant proprietor of physically abusing a Haitian immigrant customer. And, nearer the core of the 71st Police Precinct, which Flatbush shares with Crown Heights, are the alternating synagogues and churches that stake out the hotly contested territory along Eastern Parkway, where riots broke out in the summer of 1991.

I belonged to the hybrid ten percent of the population that is white, which is to say not black. The shorthand of our racial discourse allows for only these two primary categories; what corollary distinctions are then made do little to modify the harshness of this initial Manichean division. "Yellow is mellow, if you're brown stick around, when you're black get back" goes the old, ugly rhyme. The caste system it describes survives in our day and has spawned a cult of undiluted Africanness that inverts this hierarchy. Of course, virtually no one in the Western hemisphere has "pure" blood, but atavistic racial myths die hard in a culture that preaches integration but still fears or hates "the nigger in the wood-pile."

In street reality as in genealogical fact, "blackness" is both an abstraction and a spectrum. Walk in a white part of town and the deeper, modulated tones of African Americans may, to many Caucasians, seem to blur together. Perhaps it is that we who are white are taught not to stare, but to pretend that we are all alike so as not to cause embarrassment to those with darker skins, as if that were a cause for embarrassment. Or maybe it is because we are ashamed to look people in the eye whose pain and reproach and pride we cannot fully take in. But walk around the section of Flatbush where I lived and the finest gradations, blue-umber, ruddy-brown, ocher, pink, and beige, leap to the eye. There it is safe to notice that black is beautiful, ever varied but never "black."

This is an elementary observation, but conventional linguistic classification so regularly preempts perception that it is necessary to underscore it. The very essence of racism is reducing all distinctions to one. The practical test of whether this unconscious habit has become a conscious problem, subject to analysis and redress, is whether the individual in whom it appears starts to realize the myriad differences subsumed by the generally accepted single big difference. Alertness to the actual color of someone's skin in our skin color-obsessed society is therefore only the beginning. Chatting with one's neighbors in a place like Flatbush, or listening to the talk on the corner, one hears the rich accents of the deep South, the Midwest, and the Northern ghetto, along with the neutral diction of the settled bourgeoisie, the suave vowels of Jamaica, Trinidad, Grenada, the Bahamas and Guyana, and the rhythmic consonants of Haitian Creole.

The plural backgrounds evident in this catalogue are matched by diversity of other kinds. Religion plays an important role in the community and the faiths are many. Traditional and evangelical Protestant congregations continue to predominate, but a significant number of Caribbeans are Catholic and, because it runs a school system that is safe and academically strict, the church is a powerful force even among non-believers. Because of a moral authority manifest in their discipline, Muslims, belonging to several major and many smaller groups, also exert an influence greater than their number would suggest. With minimal police presence the rule in Flatbush, Muslim missionaries and security squads are often the only visible opposition to the pushers and the only organized force the gangs heed. Despite their sometime drug use—and their media images as crazed drug dealers—genuine Rastafarians are also respected for their spiritualism and self-reliance; members own several vegetarian groceries and eateries on Flatbush Avenue and their motto, "One World 360 Degrees Round," is a reassuring symbol of unity. Common to all of these denominations and sects is an essential conservatism that is rooted in the hard necessity of pulling together or holding together a community under siege.

Local cultural institutions reflect a corresponding quest for self-definition. Contrary to the blighted image of urban black life held by many outsiders, such cultural projects are proliferating in spite of scant resources. Need and respect sustain them. At the junction of Rutland Road and Flatbush Avenue is "Head-Start Books & Crafts," specializing, so its sign proclaims, in African, African-American, Hispanic, and European books. There you could find or order almost anything written by a long and ever-lengthening list of influential black writers—John Hope Franklin, Zora Neale Hurston, Chinua Achebe, James Baldwin, Aimé Césaire, Toni Morrison, Nikki Giovanni, Lerone Bennett, E. Franklin Frazier, Chester Himes, Rita Dove, W. E. B. Du Bois, Derek Walcott, Ntozake Shange, Léopold Sédar Senghor, Ralph Ellison, Marcus Garvey, Langston Hughes, Jamaica Kincaid, Ishmael Reed, Malcolm X, Harold Cruse, Paule Marshall, Amiri Baraka, and Richard Wright, to name only a few. Also in stock are volumes by a host of others less well known, augmented by Afrocentric children's books, self-help books, marriage manuals, posters, and videotapes.

All over the city, in the last several years, sidewalk tables featuring the same material have cropped up. They, in effect, are the satellites of such neighborhood centers for the dissemination of black literature, history, and social thought; in common cause they offer to the public the wealth of titles that may appear on the computers, but far less reliably on the shelves, of mainstream bookshops and chain stores. In the evening, "Head-Start's" proprietors keep the doors open for classes, reading groups, and lectures. Several blocks down, on Lincoln Road, this forum is complemented by a small gallery that exhibits paintings and sculptures by artists similarly dedicated for forging a positive self-image. Throughout the area, there are exterior murals depicting movement leaders, poets, statesmen, inventors, and the kings of Africa ending with Haile Selassie.[3] In an area rife with graffiti, these walls are honored and unblemished.

3 Editor's note: Haile Selassie I, original
    name Tafari Makonnen (1892–1975),
    emperor of Ethiopia from 1930 to 1974.

On any given day, all the many voices of the contemporary African diaspora are broadcast from hole-in-the-wall record outlets that sell classic Calypso and Reggae, or the latest Soca, Afro-pop, and hip-hop. For a time, two such shops faced each other across Flatbush Avenue and, from Friday noon into the night and on through the next day and night, you could hear Fela alternate with Flavor Flav, or Black Stalin duel vocally with the Mighty Sparrow. Occasional block parties and fairs bring dancing into the streets, and on Labor Day all of central Brooklyn descends on Eastern Parkway for the annual Caribbean Festival. While St. Patrick's Day and Columbus Day have devolved into a mix of orchestrated nostalgia, high-school jamboree, and political showcase, Brooklyn's carnival, a comparatively new but exponentially growing phenomenon, is the site of intense cultural ferment. Weeks in advance of this huge event, "mass-camps" open up in vacant store fronts all around the area. There teams of men, women, and children gather at sundown to plan their march and decorate their parade gear. Months before that, master craftsmen start work on the operatic regalia of the King, Queen, and attendants that lead each "mass-camp's" court. The preparations are done secretly so that the yearly result, with all its fanciful innovations, will come as a surprise when it finally appears before competitors and judges.

One evening several years ago, a friend and I were guided to a remote tenement basement in the heart of Crown Heights to witness the completion of one such ensemble. Made of bent and welded tubing, hammered copper amulets, cellophane, and glitter, the royal couple's towering, bird-of-paradise-like harnesses were the creation of a man who modestly would not give his full name. The day after the masquerade these glorious exoskeletons were scattered along the sidewalk like the shells of tropical insects. My first reaction when coming upon them was to think about how to lug one home. Reaching out for it, however, I hesitated, remembering the anonymous man who had spent hours making the piece, but was apparently unconcerned with its fate after the pageant.

I mention the incident because it concerns an order of things which are the topic of much art-world argument but that in Flatbush crop up as the manifestation of an old and thriving tradition. Many scholars and art critics now question the manner in which objects from other cultures are publicly displayed, for commonly they are the product of plunder from graves or sacred sites. Setting aside the moral onus of those violations, the essential dilemma of whether to exhibit such work derives from the fact that the ritual purpose they served is basic to their meaning. In many of the societies that engendered them, once that purpose was fulfilled, they ceased to be of value and were discarded. The efforts of connoisseurs to collect and preserve these intentionally perishable creations is predicated on our preoccupation with significant form, and so constitutes a fundamental misunderstanding of the esthetics of significant function. The desire to possess these creations in isolation from their fundamental context is, thus, all too often a consequence of being blind to their true beauty. Relinquishing my hold on the costume, I made contact with its informing spirit and carried that away with me.

The great complexity of the world I have tried to describe can be at least partially inferred from the details I have provided. I have spent so much time on this description—and will proceed to spend a little more—because, like the example just cited, much of what follows bears on views of the African-American community and debates about cultural diversity that take for granted a perspective that is foreign to that of the majority of my former neighbors. Their near- and long-term fate turns not on debates over political correctness in white-dominated journals but on the affinities and animosities felt by and the pressures exerted upon the various classes, creeds, and nationalities closest to home, which are complicated by the differing aspirations expressed and disillusionments endured by these individuals. Integration into white society, if regarded as worthwhile under any conditions, is not so pressing an issue as the integration or disintegration of the multicultural reality in which they already live.

Affirming black identity in the face of white indifference or hostility is not just the affair of activists, and certainly not the conceit of social theorists, but a daily struggle for collective recognition, reconciliation, and survival in which everyone is engaged without choice or exception. On the morning subway heading to Manhattan and the evening subway back to Flatbush, the woman with unguarded emotion in her face as she pores over *The Color Purple*, the testy kid with the Walkman intent on the lyrics of Public Enemy, and the man paging through Jet are all a part of that process;[4] and, they are as acutely aware of their separate passions and allegiances as they are of their shared separateness from the world in which they for the most part work. I followed the same daily path but in mental reverse. My house in Flatbush was outside the confines of my hereditary milieu, my job at The Museum of Modern Art was deep inside it. The distance covered and the inversion of vantage points such travel occasioned form the matrix of the essay that follows, since nothing makes one so aware of the contingent nature of one's sense of identity as being a commuter between two cultures. The irony of my situation was frequently pointed out to me by cabbies who would pick me up at almost any hour of the night because I am white and then peer quizzically in the mirror when I told them my homeward destination. Although some were more fearful or angrily inconvenienced than others (none expected to get a fare back to "the city"), it did not matter whether the driver was Slavic, African American, Middle Eastern, West Indian, Jewish, Italian, Asian, or WASP: nearly all of them started asking questions about how I came to live there, which soon enough turned into a lecture about why I should not. The more I explained the simple fact of having moved my family to a place I could afford in an area that was generally hospitable, the wider the gap in our understanding became. Protocol in discussions of tense

4 Editor's note: *The Color Purple* is a seminal novel by Alice Walker published in 1982. It centers on an abused African-American woman's struggle for empowerment. It won the Pulitzer Prize in 1983.

social issues demands that you let people know "where you're coming from." The flip side of this emphasis on the authenticity of one's roots is to know "your place." When I was dropped off, it was evident that however cordial the conversation had been, everything I had said was unbelievable because where I was going wasn't where I should be.

Being suspect simply as a result of being candid is a very unpleasant feeling, more unpleasant by far than the snapped heads and the trailing looks of unfamiliar stoop watchers and pedestrians who, without malice, wondered what my business in a black neighborhood was. Trying to make contact and failing is harder to dismiss than passing through like a stranger, especially when it happens that their turf is also yours. Within my unevenly marbled neighborhood, preconceptions about who belonged and who did not set the stage for all manner of misapprehensions. Every encounter was loaded with so many psychological and social expectations and with such a wellspring of hurt and skepticism that its meaning might be simultaneously found and lost, Rashomon-like, in the almost inevitably conflicting impressions that the participants took away.

An example: at a school Halloween party, my then six-year-old daughter had herself made up to look like a cat by an older—incidentally African-American—girl, who overzealously covered her entire face with a thick coat of charcoal grease. Walking home afterwards we crossed paths with a West Indian woman and her daughter, who looked at us first with curiosity, then disbelief, then anger, having apparently concluded that my child was in blackface and so mocking their complexion. There was nothing I could say to ease the tension that would not compound it. Thus, the overriding condition of life where cultures meet on an unequal footing is the unreliability of the signals one sends and the unpredictability of the responses one gets. No one trusts absolutely, or even very much, in the good intentions of the other. Without warning, appearances may betray the truth of a situation, setting off chain reactions of misunderstanding that end up becoming its truth.

If signs like these could be so easily misconstrued, or if my words rang dissonantly or false in the minds of taxi drivers, they also frequently fell on uncomprehending ears of many of my professional colleagues or, worse, evoked something exotic, as though I were telling a running tale of life on the wild side. Almost impossible to communicate were the ordinary subtleties of the circumstances I tried to describe. Still, my situation was exceptional only to the degree that its contradictions and confusions were on a daily basis obvious and inescapable; otherwise, it was merely symptomatic of the larger process of America's uncertain social and cultural evolution with which we all must reckon.

Having had to deal with the constant perplexity and sometime pain of being marginalized within my community, I had no misconception about the resemblance of my predicament to that of my black neighbors. Being a self-elected minority within a "minority" is not the same as being an involuntary minority within a disproportionately large and powerful majority. Never did I try to "blend in." A case in point: the part Hispanic "white" boy, in his mid-teens, who tended the corner grocery and secretly listened to Mozart, gradually affected a deep Trenchtown Jamaican accent; he had a good musical ear and sincerely wanted to sound like the people he served. Among whites caught between racial camps, the desire to live "black" is a recurrent syndrome that only heightens awareness of the telling incongruity between style and substance, manners and motivation. A parallel belief that one can learn by impersonation how it feels to be different from what one is has arisen among naively sympathetic liberals. But humanity is an historical and cultural aggregate that will not yield its complex nature to gross humanist generalization, however well-intended. Far from showing solidarity, stressing superficial similarities between people or attempting to stand in another person's shoes is, if anything, an insult.

Among the whitest of whites in the vicinity, I was too conspicuous to even entertain such illusions. An almost comically visible man, the only thing I shared with Ralph Ellison's invisible protagonist was a measure of self-consciousness about my race that transcended immediate concerns about how to get through the day and made me wonder at the endless and absurd ramifications of this one unalterable fact. Nonetheless, with the passage of time, it became increasingly apparent that I was not an internal expatriate but the uneasy inhabitant of a sequestered region of what has long been and still is an essential part of my own culture. For, in addition to the many aspects of our original heritages that have been absorbed, exchanged, and transformed by living side by side if not together, blacks and whites in America have developed a unique if often harrowing consciousness directly out of their long, difficult history of proximity. The scarred fruits of that special consciousness are our dearly paid-for common wealth.

As this conviction has deepened, it has become ever clear to me that segregation in this country is not just a matter of divorcing ourselves physically from one another; nor does it always flow from or confirm ill-will. As much as anything, it results from a failure to articulate the fullness of the things we have experienced and to envision clearly the obstacles we have yet to and may never completely overcome. In short, it is a failure of the imagination, which is the theme of Part II, which follows.

Since completing this text, I have left Flatbush for reasons of safety. Four years ago last May, a fifteen-year-old boy armed with an automatic pistol stopped his bike in the middle of the street outside our house and fired down the block, grievously wounding another fifteen-year-old boy who was standing on the corner. By the time I got to the door, the shooter had calmly remounted and ridden off without interference. No one dared take him on. I could never find out if the victim survived, but as I walked away from where he lay bleeding on the pavement, tended by his mother and surrounded by onlookers, I heard his brother come up the sidewalk, yelling that he knew who had done it and was going to kill him. I do not know if he ever did, or if the police ever arrested the suspect.

In the following years, such violence became terrifyingly commonplace, largely as a result of the ready availability of crack and handguns. A bodega owner and the local shoemaker were shot in daylight hours; men would stumble out of the drug-infested buildings bleeding from puncture wounds; fusillades were heard almost every summer night; and it was not unusual for helicopters to hover after dark, shining spotlights onto roofs and into backyards in search of someone on the run. When I talked to my seven-year-old daughter about moving, she cried and said there was no need since she knew just what to do when there were shots outside: get down on the floor until they stopped. It was time to go.

Most of the people we left behind understood our departure. Many had wanted to leave for years but could not abandon their lifetime homes, or could not afford to buy another, even with the increased resale value of the one they had owned for so long. Their good-byes were warm but tinged with sorrowful frustration. Others resented outright our pulling up stakes, and for some that resentment flowed out of the oldest and deepest of suspicions. We were community deserters, but more than that, it proved that we were just like other whites after all. An elderly woman who until that time had always said a cheerful good morning and had occasionally stopped to chat, walked away after overhearing the news from a mutual friend, muttering in stage whisper, "Well, you never liked us anyway."

Much of this section, as well as Part II, was drafted before that day and before I had any intention or any opportunity to go elsewhere. Some sections are revised versions of shorter pieces, while the balance was written to record experiences and feelings that I knew would change in memory and as my situation changed. So it has. My involvement in the day-to-day dynamics of racial and cultural diversity is different now that I live in an area integrated in almost exactly the opposite proportion as Flatbush. My sources of information are different and on the whole less reliable and less well-balanced. The social distance I once traveled daily can now only be bridged by the things I read and see, which makes me evermore alert to and dissatisfied by the restricted access to black culture in the mainstream media and the general misrepresentation of the context in which it flourishes. My stake in greater openness and inclusiveness continues to be personal; I do not want and I cannot afford to be cut off from so essential a part of my world.

Part II

White Americans have supposed "Europe" and "civilization" to be synonyms—which they are not—and have been distrustful of other standards and other sources of vitality, especially those produced in America itself … What it comes down to is that if we, who can scarcely be considered a white nation, persist in thinking of ourselves as one, we condemn ourselves … to sterility and decay, whereas if we could accept ourselves as we are we might bring new life to Western achievements and transform them.
— James Baldwin[5]

More than any other institution, The Museum of Modern Art has for generations publicly defined modernism's essential character and scope. From the outset, MoMA's perspective was internationalist and its approach encyclopedic as well as evolutionary. In the effort to establish the modernist canon, MoMA's founder, Alfred H. Barr, Jr., took it upon himself and his collaborators to look wherever the fertile conditions for modern art existed and wherever examples were reported (**plates 1** and **2**).[6] Although many factors influenced how that ambition was pursued in practice and significant oversight certainly did occur, the belief that modernism was a multifaceted phenomenon was a decisive criterion of Barr's endeavor.

Barr thus devoted his energies to collecting and researching not only the now-acknowledged classics of the tradition—Paul Cézanne, Georges Seurat, Vincent van Gogh, Pablo Picasso, Henri Matisse, Piet Mondrian, Paul Klee, Vasily Kandinsky, Kazimir Malevich and so on—but also championed work from farther afield esthetically though sometimes closer to home geographically. For

5 James Baldwin, "The Fire Next Time," in *The Price of the Ticket: Collected Non-Fiction, 1948–1985* (Michael Joseph, London, 1985), p.375.

6 Editor's note: Alfred H. Barr, Jr. (1902–1981), American art historian, curator, and founding director of The Museum of Modern Art, New York.

example, the museum's abiding if intermittently active interest in Latin American art no doubt owed a good deal to reasons of State, as its critics have claimed, but it also testified to the variety and importance of the modernist tendencies south of our borders, and Barr's prompt acknowledgement of them. When MoMA most ardently presented and collected Mexican art (**plates 5** and **6**), José Clemente Orozco (**plate 3**), Diego Rivera, and David Alfaro Siqueiros were commanding models across the United States and not, as they are now often described, mere precursors to the Abstract Expressionists.[7] As it happened, Barr had first met Rivera in Russia in 1928, a year before MoMA was founded, and the muralist was the subject of one of the fifteen exhibitions devoted to Latin American art mounted by MoMA between 1929 and 1945 (**plate 4**).[8] Awareness of Latin America peaked as a result of the hemispheric entrenchment imposed by the war in Europe, and by 1943 the permanent collection of the museum included some 293 Latin American works. Although institutional interest subsequently flagged, by 1974 the museum's Latin American holdings had nevertheless increased to 650, thanks to a fund especially established for the purpose.[9]

Among this number were paintings by Frida Kahlo, which languished in storage for much of the last forty years. Only recently were they rescued from limbo and returned to the walls on a regular

7   Editor's note: notably, in 1940 MoMA commissioned from Orozco a fresco for inclusion in the exhibition *Twenty Centuries of Mexican Art* (15 May – 30 September 1940). As part of the presentation, Orozco painted the six-panel fresco *Dive Bomber and Tank* (1940) over a period of ten days, often in front of the viewing public.

8   Editor's note: this is the exhibition *Diego Rivera*, MoMA, New York (22 December 1931 – 27 January 1932). The museum brought Diego Rivera to New York six weeks before the show's opening to paint "portable murals" for the exhibition, providing him with a makeshift studio in the gallery. He painted five frescoes on moveable supports of steel, cement, and plaster, chief among them *Liberation of the Peon*, *Sugar Cane*, and *Agrarian Leader Zapata* (all 1931).

9   I owe much of the information pertaining to Barr's collecting policies and early programming of The Museum of Modern Art to the research of Rona Roob, archivist of The Alfred H. Barr, Jr. Papers at the museum. Her published findings often appear in the museum's quarterly journal *MoMA Magazine*. See, for example: Rona Roob, "From the Archives: The Museum and Latin American Art." *MoMA Magazine* (Summer 1993), p.16.

basis. Changing tastes have so catapulted this neglected artist's reputation that current acquisition of her work would have put a significant strain on even MoMA's resources. A further, though more obscure, example of Barr's risk-taking broad-mindedness has similar significance. Following his 1944 trip to Cuba, Barr arranged for a small show of contemporary Cuban art, for which he wrote the catalogue and from which he acquired several works for the museum's permanent collection. A recent exhibition devoted to Wifredo Lam and his artistic affinities at the Studio Museum in Harlem (**plate 8**) centered on the Cuban painter's huge gouache *The Jungle* (1943), which has long hung in MoMA's lobby, and also drew on Barr's other finds.[10] Granted, few of these paintings have retained their freshness, but their inclusion in the collection is a testament to Barr's willingness to gamble on his taste and on the talent of non-mainstream artists. Meanwhile, the presence of these works in New York made it possible to reconsider the sources of an Afro-Asian painter primarily viewed as a disciple of European Surrealism, and to do so not as a revisionist gambit but to correct the record according to the evidence that Barr, as both connoisseur and art historian, had gathered.

Parallel to Barr's involvement in Latin American art (**plate 7**) was the attention he paid to tribal and folk art, which was frequently integrated into MoMA's programs during the first decade and a half of its existence. Generally, this interest was prompted by such work's direct historical influence on major modernist movements such as Cubism and Expressionism, as was the case with the 1935 exhibition *African Negro Art* (**plate 9**).[11] On other occasions, such as the 1937 show of the African-American stone carver William Edmondson (**plates 10** and **11**), the emphasis was on such tradition-based art's indirect formal correspondence with these same movements.[12]

10 Editor's note: the exhibition in question is *Wifredo Lam and His Contemporaries, 1938–1952,* Studio Museum in Harlem, 6 December 1992 – 11 April 1993.

11 Editor's note: the exhibition titled *African Negro Art* ran at The Museum of Modern Art, New York from 18 March to 19 May 1935.

12 Editor's note: the exhibition *Sculpture by William Edmondson* ran at The Museum of Modern Art, New York from 20 October to 1 December 1937.

Under Barr's direction, the museum also mounted exhibitions devoted to American folk art in 1933 and 1938.[13] Shortly after, it hosted *Indian Art of the United States* (1941; **plate 12**), co-curated by René d'Harnoncourt, later director of the museum; *Religious Folk Art of the Southwest* (1943), a traveling show recast for MoMA by Dorothy Miller, Barr's closest colleague, in which all of the work was Hispanic in origin; *Joe Milone's Shoe Shine Stand* (1943; **plate 13**), a local vernacular construction brought to Barr's attention by Louise Nevelson; and a retrospective of the "naif" painter Morris Hirshfield (1943), organized by dealer Sidney Janis.[14]

Barr's eagerness to show the reach of modernism beyond the established cultural centers extended to his careful recording of the national origins of artists in MoMA's collection. In addition to those who were American and European-born, Barr's 1945 index cited Argentines, Chileans, Colombians, Cubans, Ecuadorians, Haitians, Mexicans, Peruvians, and Uruguayans. In 1948, Australians, Bolivians, Brazilians, and Guatemalans were included; in 1958, Japanese, South Africans, and Venezuelans joined the list; and in Barr's 1967 update, artists from Algeria, Canada, China, Ethiopia, Iceland, India, Iran, Israel, Korea, Kuwait, Lebanon, Morocco, Nicaragua, Paraguay, Puerto Rico, Rhodesia, Sudan, Tanzania, Tunisia, Turkey, and Uganda were added. Though some of these artists made their careers in Paris, New York, or other such capitals, many had not. Their presence, therefore, reflected both Barr's catholic interests and his adventurousness. As in the case of the Cuban material, work from Africa was acquired in the process of his searching for art where it was made.

---

13 Editor's note: *Exhibition of American Folk Art*, The Museum of Modern Art, New York, 30 November 1932 – 15 January 1933; *American Folk Art*, The Museum of Modern Art, New York, 2 February – 7 March 1938.

14 Editor's note: the MoMA exhibitions in question are: *Indian Art of the United States* (22 January – 27 April 1941), co-curated by René d'Harnoncourt and Frederic H. Douglas; *Religious Folk Art of the Southwest* (28 April – 13 June 1943); *Joe Milone's Shoe Shine Stand* (22 December 1942 – 10 January 1943); and *The Paintings of Morris Hirshfield* (23 June – 1 August 1943).

In light of the current condemnations of multiculturalism and the published demands for the resignation or firing of museum professionals actively engaged in the promotion of diversity, it is necessary to recall that Barr's patrons were at crucial times impatient with or intolerant of his experiments and excursions. In late 1943, after having upset several trustees—in particular, the esthetically conservative board chairman Stephen C. Clark—by offering museum space and sanction to the Hirshfield show, and by installing Joe Milone's richly ornamented shoeshine stand in the museum's lobby, Barr was fired as the museum's director. Barr's dismissal came little more than a week after Victor D'Amico, the pioneering head of MoMA's Education Department, inaugurated an exhibition of work by students at the Hampton Institute entitled *Young Negro Art*.[15]

With the exception of the museum's 1944 exhibitions *Modern Cuban Painters* and *Paintings by Jacob Lawrence* (**plate 14**), Barr's departure broke MoMA's tradition of culturally varied fare for years to come.[16] Although he returned to the institution in 1947 as director of the museum's collections and served for another twenty

15 Editor's note: Victor D'Amico (1904–1987), American teaching artist and educator. He was a pioneer of modern art education and the founding director of the Department of Education at The Museum of Modern Art, New York. He believed "that the arts are a humanizing force and that their major function is to vitalize living."

 The exhibition *Young Negro Art* ran at The Museum of Modern Art, New York from 26 October to 28 November 1943.

16 The stated rationales for some of these exhibitions, *Young Negro Art* in particular, have a paternalistic ring to them, but that must be measured against the sheer fact that such shows occurred at all, and did so years before the broad national mandate arising out of the Civil Rights movement. Other texts merit rereading in light of more recent polemics concerning the purely formal treatment of tribal arts advocated by some modernist critics versus the more complex approach to this material provided by others.

After a quotation in the press release from Eleanor Roosevelt's foreword to the catalogue of *Indian Art of the United States* (1941), the show's curators Frederic H. Douglas and René D'Harnoncourt stated: "Fine art in the sense of art for art's sake is a concept that is almost unknown in Indian cultures. There are very few aboriginal art forms that have no established function in tribal life .... The close relationship between esthetic and technical perfection gives the work of most Indian artists a basic unity rarely found in the product of an urban civilization .... Beyond general statements little can be said about Indian art that would fit all the various tribes and tribal groups, since each area of Indian culture has an art of its own." These attitudes are more enlightened than much that currently appears in print regarding the cultural specificity and function of non-mainstream art; the fact that such ideas were discussed in the context of MoMA's other programming gives some

years, Barr never again fully resumed the position he had once occupied as MoMA's guiding hand. Now almost universally honored for his curatorial prescience and ingenuity, Barr is rightly held up as a model for generations of his successors. When it comes to the issue of cultural diversity, MoMA has much to be proud of and virtually all of it resulted from Barr's proactive rather than reactive engagement with the problems and material involved. Preferring to ratify their own conservative view of modernism, however, some of his ostensible admirers conveniently forget the liberality of his pioneering approach to collecting and museum programming and take for granted its lasting consequences.

All of this is preamble to the present resurgence of pluralist thinking and pluralist demands. What is notable about Barr is that he was a pluralist by choice, or rather his exacting curiosity and the range of works that attracted his attention compelled him to that conclusion. Instead of being responsive to external forces, he responded internally and spontaneously to the disparate array of art in which he divined intrinsic merit and patterns of affinity. His judgment of quality was therefore specific before it was categorical, and when in doubt he opted for critical openness rather than the pretense of critical infallibility.

In the years since his retirement and death, and even before, the American view of modernism became narrower not broader as American art gained in authority and its institutional base

indication of what was lost when, in the course of institutional evolution, the consideration of vernacular or non-Western art of all kinds—tribal, folk, and classical—was shifted over to specialized museums such as The Museum of Primitive Art, The Museum of Folk Art, the Americas Society, Asia House, and others [in New York]. Much later, in 1967, when René D'Harnoncourt was still director of MoMA—that is, before the brief, socially crusading tenures of Bates Lowry and John B. Hightower—the members of the museum's Junior Council met and founded what was to become the Studio Museum in Harlem, having already initiated a series of outreach programs directed toward the African-American community involving both white and black artists and educators. To be sure, MoMA could not have continued forever to embrace the full range of work that Barr originally addressed—nor could it have kept fully abreast of all new work shown by focused museums such as the Studio Museum in Harlem—but the division of labor that resulted has undeniably had its narrowing effects on theoretical presentations of modern art.

expanded. During the 1960s and 1970s historians and critics streamlined the famously churning diagram of the course of modern art history that Barr had devised in 1936; and, to an increasing degree, they concentrated on a strictly, often mechanically formal interpretation of the art they deemed worthy of that tightly channeled "mainstream." The break with the founding spirit of MoMA came with this triumph of American formalism, and not with the so-called postmodernist reaction to it. Ironically, the rebellion against modernism as it thus came to be narrowly defined, while often interpreted as a demand that the museum reject the whole of its tradition, in many respects challenges the institution and others modeled on it to do the reverse, and return to that tradition's generative spirit and empirical approach.

I arrived at MoMA at just the moment when the old dogmas were imploding under pressure from critical theory, while being exploded by eclectic contemporary artistic practices that they could neither explain, accommodate, nor constrain. These combined forces have pushed MoMA back into the open field of cultural debate, a terrain made treacherous by impending social and political confrontations of far greater magnitude. After the speculation-driven boom of the 1980s, the art world has found itself confronting a definite bust. As material circumstances have worsened and public patience has frayed, anger at the institutions identified with monied privilege and resentment over decades of officially sanctioned indifference to marginalized groups have grown.

For the second time in a quarter century, the country, in general, and museums, in particular, are being forced to reckon the costs of squandering an interlude of prosperity and civil peace. And once again, we are being brought back to the unfinished business of forming a polity and a culture out of a heterogeneous population that is celebrated in patriotic myth but whose actual distinctions are regularly ignored if not disdained. The fault line between the black and white worlds is both symbolic of this incomplete social fusion and the single most intractable impediment to overall cohesion. Despite legal and economic advances that have generally benefited the African-American middle class, that gap has widened rather than closed. It has done so not only because of the deteriorating conditions of the inner city, the gradual erosion of our global economic advantage, and a loss of national nerve, but also because, with tempers shorter than ever, the very terms employed to describe this dangerous state of affairs are themselves in dispute.

The debate about multiculturalism is, in that measure, a fight over words. Skirmishes about acceptable nomenclature have proven that any term is a provocation when employed as a euphemism for attitudes the speaker has not examined or hopes to hide. "Minorities" rightly question the term and its connotations because in other parts of the world they are majorities. "Third world" people understandably object to the hierarchical meanings that have attached themselves to this once purely geopolitical phrase. "The Other," so called by ostensibly sympathetic theorists, increasingly balk at having their variousness dissolved into a collective abstraction whose sole characteristic is being "other than" whatever the dominant social entity happens to be. "People of color" increasingly doubt the benefits of such an ambiguous turn of phrase; after all, as an Hispanic artist recently pointed out at a panel I attended, it's really just a cumbersome way of saying "colored people."

From what one group calls another, the problem extends to what any collectivity calls itself. Depending on age, attitude, or circumstance, a person in my old neighborhood of Flatbush might identify themselves as a Black, an African American, a Negro, or, as is defiantly common on the streets and among a younger generation of rappers and comedians—a Nigger. Over the years, the rotation of these usages, and the shift back and forth between their positive and negative interpretation, has been a chief indicator of changing racial sensitivities. This need to keep revising or exchanging vocabulary testifies to the basic unreliability of language in relation to its social function. On all sides, our inability to speak about or name the chronic condition from which we suffer is a principal source of our discomfort. We cannot say what ails us because the very phrases we use are at once symptoms and aggravating factors of that condition. Nevertheless, like any physical pain, the sharp pang we feel on hearing or speaking some words is an urgent and healthy reminder of the fundamentally unattended causes of our plight.

Proliferating attempts at formulating a semantic balm for raw social sores have in the meantime provided endless amusement to commentators of a disenchanted-liberal to conservative bent. Double-speak is always fair game, of course, and without question there has been ample foolishness to fuel the satirists' fancy. Anecdotes of loony self-righteousness are a staple of conservative complaints in the same way that talk of welfare-queens driving Cadillacs once highlighted warnings about the folly of providing economic subsidies to the poor. On the whole, however, the eager debunking of "politically correct" speech has offered journalistic cheap thrills while simultaneously providing an alibi for those anxious to evade serious engagement with the underlying issues. In short, it is a way of ruling out discussion by incessantly calling verbal fouls.

Formerly a self-critical part of radical left-wing parlance, the label "P.C." [political correctness] is of a more sinister convenience to the radical Right. Suggesting rote agreement among members of every stirring social group when in reality there is none, at the same time implying a policed intellectual Left at a time when the Left has all but ceased to exist as a coherent force, the epithet "P.C.," as it has been misappropriated and promiscuously applied by the far Right, effectively supplants a contentious and yet-to-be-defined mass of people and body of thought with the image of a threatening new conformity.

Above all, conservatives recoil from pluralism because it means accepting a world that is in constant flux. In order to persuade people of the dangers of change, the Right conjures up the opposite of the diversity it actually dreads—that is, a monolithic, undifferentiated alien horde making unfair demands on an innocent, individualistic Everyman. Alternatives to conventional wisdom are regarded as proof of a conspiracy of "them" against "us," and the ensuing confrontation is an ideological civil war between "our" common sense and time-honored beliefs and "their" mysterious and irrational creeds. Correspondingly, the mention of multiculturalism has come to evoke the Red Menace, the Yellow Peril, Black Rage, and the Spanish Inquisition all rolled into one. By the same chain of unreason, the derisive use of the term "P.C." has been transformed into the ultimate semantic weapon for ridiculing and denying the lively dissimilarity among people and their views; it is bigotry by abbreviation.

By rapid rhetorical contagion, "P.C." has thus become the new omnibus taboo. The term's broad appeal derives from genuine frustration as much as from polemical opportunism. Many, who would like to think well of themselves, at least to the extent that they do not in general think badly of others, feel unfairly called to judgment by those drawing attention to the denigrating assumptions and disastrous consequences of "benign neglect" in all dimensions of our public life.[17] Among those professionally or otherwise committed

17 The expression "benign neglect" is a direct reference to the policy on racial matters proposed by Harvard-based social scientist and subsequently United States Ambassador to the United Nations (1975–76) as well as United States Senator (1977–2001) Daniel Patrick Moynihan, when he served as counselor to the Richard Nixon Republican administration (in 1969–70) despite his prominence in the Democratic Party. On 1 March 1970, the front page of *The New York Times* first reported that in a memorandum (dated 16 January 1970) Moynihan had advised President Nixon that "the issue of race in the United States could benefit from a period of 'benign neglect'." According to Moynihan, the U.S. government's focus on racial problems actually helped stoke them and in his report he recommended Nixon to exercise "benign neglect" to "avoid situations in which extremists of either race are given opportunities for martyrdom, heroics, histrionics, and whatever." See Peter Kihss, "'Benign Neglect' on Race Is Proposed by Moynihan," *The New York Times* (1 March 1970). More generally, Moynihan's advice to conservatives voiced the battle fatigue of many liberal constituencies in the white establishment that had been eclipsed by more radical tendencies in the Black Power and Anti-War movements of the 1960s. In truth, Moynihan's recommendation signaled a retreat from the ongoing struggle to undo generations of institutional racism by privileged middle-of-the-roaders. Worse, it foreshadowed the willingness of many in their ranks to collaborate in the epochal reactionary rollbacks of the Nixon, Reagan, Bush, and Trump eras.

to philanthropic enterprises, this sense of personal disorientation is sometimes exacerbated by fear and resentment that good works undertaken in good faith will or have become counters in a struggle for power among factions who may have no loyalty to or investment in the institutions that are the temporary site of their crusade.

There is also the matter of styles of cultural consumption. In reading rooms, silence prevails while books argue; in museums, which are the public libraries of visual culture, people reverently contemplate works of art that often quarrel with one another's poetic or philosophical rationale. In these places, it is expected that intellectual and artistic cacophony will be met with quiet appreciation. When those conflicting views are echoed aloud and amplified by a citizenry rarely heard from in or outside such establishments, that church-like decorum is broken. As accustomed to the disruptive mobbing of "blockbuster" exhibitions as museums have become, they still find it hard to deal with people who identify "too" strongly with what they see or react "too" directly to what perplexes or disturbs them. Hybrid in its origins, multiform in its realization, and arguable in its import, modern art was made for controversy; for the most part, however, the institutions created to house and display it are ill-prepared to be forums for that controversy when it inevitably erupts.

Never was this more uncomfortably obvious than in the 1960s and early 1970s. During the sharp waning spasms of the Civil Rights and Black Power movements and the Vietnam War protests, major museums were frequently the focus of demonstrations and the locus of mostly ill-fated experiments aimed at broadening their audience and artistic purview and making their programs more "relevant." Enthusiasm for reform or institutional activism soon withered in the face of guerrilla actions and expressions of defiance that were more startling than threatening but that still managed to undermine confidence among patrons and interested members of the public that the protesters had any respect for the esthetic and intellectual values they cherished. It was a short jump for hysterics to assume that the art-world agitators were essentially illiterate iconoclasts bent on destruction for its own sake: if they changed slogans or made agitprop posters, so the logic went, they must be deaf to T. S. Eliot and blind to Henri Matisse.

Within the beleaguered pro-modernist old guard, many, once militant in their own day and for their own causes, were appalled by what they perceived as a fall from the idealistic grace of the ideological battles of the 1930s, 1940s, and 1950s. From their ranks came many of today's chief neo-conservative advocates and apologists, determined to defend the ground they had long ago won as artistic and social progressives against all newcomers inspired by the tradition of which they still claim to be the exclusive representatives. Having lost control of artistic and social discourse in the 1960s and 1970s, such aging warriors retreated from the fertile chaos of the contemporary scene to their various professional citadels to nurse their bruises and plot their revenge. Widely broadcast from these far-flung redoubts, their obsessional contempt for the partisans of cultural diversity set the tone for a rising generation of younger conservatives. Having missed the social and artistic crucible experienced by old and new vanguardists alike, the young conservatives of the 1980s fed upon canned images of bad political theater, from gun-toting students at Ivy League colleges to Leonard Bernstein's infamous party for the Black Panthers.

Besides making them prematurely dyspeptic, this diet of outdated radical chic convinced converts to cultural reaction that the exigencies and expediencies of the "real" world were entirely incompatible with esthetic activity. Having no stomach for contradiction and no understanding of how it fuels the creative process, they argued that formal and philosophical purity must be protected at all costs from contamination by social impurities. To be sure, the cause of art-for-art's sake is hardly new; nor is it inherently wrong-headed. Motivated by the positive if illusory ambition of completely transforming life by art or life into art, total immersion in the esthetic is one of the exhilarating constants of modernist thinking from Charles Baudelaire to Oscar Wilde to John Cage—all of whom were worldly indeed. The pessimistic and backward-looking version of this same impulse is another thing entirely, since it constricts imaginative freedom in both the artistic and the social domain. Maintenance rather than creation becomes the sole objective; passive longing for the Golden Age coupled with active hostility toward an unruly present consume the spirit and skew the mind.

The dichotomous concept of the imagination supposed by this negative estheticism also assumes that all true artists have the luxury of removing themselves from mundane circumstances and struggles to compose their disinterested thoughts or images. If not an aristocracy of talent in the old sense, this view posits a protected cultural meritocracy, where the worthy are guaranteed sufficient material and mental security to insulate them from "extra-artistic" distraction. Utterly ignored by this approach are the artists whose subject is, in fact, the impossibility of taking refuge in their thoughts or existing comfortably in the world as they find it. At regular intervals in its history, modernism's direction has been altered by individual as well as organized efforts to reflect upon and examine this exact dilemma. Some of the work has been overtly political in form and content but much has not been, though it has been deeply rooted in social realities without which the art makes no sense at all. Recent events have recast this problem and revived interest in these precedents. The new work that addresses art's critical relation to its context thus fruitfully complicates the task faced by museums dedicated to deepening public understanding of modernism's continued development in our day.

It is no accident that African-American artists count prominently among those caught between esthetic dreams deferred and wide-awake nightmares. One of these artists is Adrian Piper. Over the last several years, Piper has created a series of installations that probe many of the aforementioned issues. *Cornered* (1988; **plate**

15), for example, is a self-portrait of the artist as racial enigma. This installation consists of a single video monitor positioned defensively in a corner of the space in which it is presented and behind an overturned table. In the video, which is the centerpiece of the work, Piper, assuming a politely insistent schoolmarmish tone, speaks directly to the viewer and describes how she is often mistaken for white because of the fairness of her skin and the double-bind of being privy to what whites say when they think no blacks are around. In the course of her talk, she states: "... I have no choice. I'm cornered. If I tell you who I am, you become nervous and uncomfortable or antagonized. But if I don't tell you who I am, then I have to pass for white, and why should I have to do that?" Further calling into question the visual fictions of "whiteness" and "blackness," Piper's installation includes her father's two birth certificates, one identifying him as "white" and the other as "octoroon" (a historical term for fair-skinned African Americans). Framed, the certificates hang on the wall, one at each side of the monitor. In the course of her talk, Piper explains how her father came to have two birth certificates, which gave him the option to "pass." She then points out that, given the long history of interbreeding in this country, no one can be confident of their ethnic purity and therefore everyone either knowingly or unknowingly shares her and her father's ambiguous status. The theme is further explored in the seventeen-channel video installation *Out of the Corner* (1990; **plate 16**). In it, sixteen monitors form a barricade in front of a single monitor, which is placed in the corner of a room behind an overturned table. In the single corner monitor, Piper addresses the viewer speaking on the logic of miscegenation, while in the other monitors the theme is reiterated by a chorus of voices—whose sixteen speakers, one figure per monitor, are all apparently white. Appearing on the screens, they repeat, "Some of my female ancestors were so-called 'house niggers' who were raped by their white slave masters. If you are an American, some of yours probably were too." Around the periphery of the room, on the walls hang at eye-level sixty-four black-and-white photographs of African-American women from different social backgrounds that the artist rephotographed from *Ebony* magazine. Each face is recognizably black, yet different in skin tone, "Negroid" features, dress, and make-up.

Avowedly didactic, Piper takes a Minimalist adaptation of mathematical Set Theory and applies it to social and racial classifications, in this case diagramming the permutations of a racial paradigm the way Sol LeWitt dismantled and displayed all the structural subdivisions of a standard geometric cube. And like LeWitt's work, it makes one fundamentally reconceive the object of one's attention, where before one looked only in order to confirm a prior definition of that object. Piper's response to the conceptual inquiries of LeWitt—for whom she worked as an assistant early in her career—goes much further than formal methodology and delves into the problems of esthetic idealism.

Another of her recent installations addresses the matter head-on. Entitled *What It's Like, What It Is #3* (1991; **plate 17**), the piece was commissioned for *DIS*LOCATIONS, my first curatorial project at The Museum of Modern Art.[18] It consists of a tiered geometric structure—one reminiscent of Minimalist sculptures of the 1960s and 1970s and at the same time evoking a pristine amphitheater of sorts— with bleacher seating on all four sides, rising to a height of about seven feet. Mounted on the wall just above the uppermost step of the structure, a ribbon of mirrors runs around the room. In the middle of the small amphitheater is a tall box. A video screen, level with the mirrors, is set into the top of each of the box's four facets. At MoMA, every surface in the room, including the tall box, the ceiling, and the squared-off floor, was painted the same hard white, made brighter still by an overhead grid of naked, high-intensity spotlights.

---

18 Editor's note: *DISLOCATIONS*, a group show organized by Robert Storr, The Museum of Modern Art, New York, 20 October 1991 – 7 January 1992. It presented seven installations in all, respectively by Louise Bourgeois, Chris Burden, Sophie Calle, David Hammons, Ilya Kabakov, Bruce Nauman, and Adrian Piper.

Spectators entered through a narrow cut in the corner of the structure, and were free to climb the bleachers and to sit anywhere. As they came and went and changed places, taking the measure of the space and notice of one another, a man's head appeared on the screen. Shot from the left, right, front, and back, he appeared in the round as if trapped inside the vertical box. At intervals he would shift his head to the right, rotating like a lighthouse beacon and seemingly casting his glance on each side of the room and on everyone in it, though in fact his gaze met his own eyes reflected in the mirrors on the surrounding walls of the room. Against the rising and falling of an exultant soul song—from all sides came music and, faint behind it, the noise of a crowd—the man, who was young, quiet in demeanor, and black, would haltingly, wincingly repeat, "I'm not pushy, I'm not sneaky, I'm not lazy, I'm not noisy, I'm not vulgar, I'm not rowdy, I'm not horny, I'm not scary, I'm not shiftless, I'm not crazy, I'm not servile, I'm not stupid, I'm not dirty, I'm not smelly, I'm not childish, I'm not evil." At the end of this litany, which represents a partial list of negative characteristics ascribed to his "kind," his eyelids fluttered and closed as if he could no longer bear to see or be seen, and his head dropped away into darkness.

Reaction to *DIS*LOCATIONS was mixed, but the brunt of the negative response fell on three of the seven works with an explicitly political aspect; Piper's installation was several times singled out for complaint. Speaking to, and presumably for, this hostile constituency, one critic concluded, "Upstairs, though, the installations can be summed up in a sentence or two, and looking at them isn't very different from reading about them .... In the center of the amphitheater is a blue pillar with a television screen on each face, and on each screen runs a videotape of a black man chanting, 'I'm...not...stupid,' 'I'm...not...horny,' etc. You sit down on one of the tiers in the amphitheater and watch the tape, and that's the piece. The point of [the] piece is exactly as obvious as it seems."[19]

19 Adam Gopnik, "The Art World: Empty Frames," *The New Yorker*, 25 November 1991 issue, pp.110–120.

Setting aside the self-disqualifying observation of a writer who glibly asserts that "looking at [the work] isn't very different from reading about [it]" and then misinforms his readers about the "blue pillar" at the center of the all-white room, the crux of this appraisal lies in its telling critical mistakes and oversights. Evidently predisposed to judge all art "with a message" as crudely moralizing and esthetically obvious, the reviewer concentrated solely on the "message" spoken from the video monitor, assuming that the audience to whom it was being delivered was racially enlightened and predominantly white, in which case the man on the screen was preaching to the liberal choir while exploiting their vestigial guilt.

The issue in this review, and several like it, was not, after all, Piper's simplistic notion of her artistic mission, but rather what Ezra Pound called the "ambition of the reader," which in the text cited was damningly low. Unfortunately, inattentiveness on the part of such expert readers-turned-writers tends to diminish curiosity in their lay following. Insofar as that audience already shared similar assumptions about the make-up of the museum public and the ethical self-satisfaction of socially oriented art, those attitudes quite literally colored the reactions of people who, had they been encouraged to analyze their personal experience fully, might have arrived at a distinctly different assessment of a situation in which they had an active part to play.

Take away these preconceptions—which, unwittingly, have all the practical consequences of overt prejudice—and the dynamic relations of the elements in Piper's installation are altered dramatically. Consider, for starters, that rather than lecturing the people in the room, the man in the box was engaged in a monologue. Consider also—all the while remembering that the performer was embodying character and not just mouthing the scripted opinions of the artist— that this man was at least as focused on the bitter inner resonance of his words and their outwardly reflected expression as he was upon being witnessed by or bearing witness to those gathered round. Further, suppose that while listening to his voice, the eyes of individual spectators drifted away from the video image, fell skittishly on faces next to or across from them, then wandered up to the mirrors in which their own gaze was captured and multiplied, along with that of everyone else present including the man on the screen, so that altogether in each other's sight they became a crowd. Factor into that optically tessellated group a number of African Americans, and envision the looks they exchanged among themselves and with their non-African-American neighbors as they simultaneously heard the repeated slurs and repeated denials. Then let the balance shift, so that a few whites are scattered among many blacks in the blanched chamber resounding with the bitter voice. Or, as was in fact the case one day [at MoMA] when I went in to check on things, picture a group of teenage boys from Harlem sitting by themselves in the same space, attending to the same hurtful phrases articulated by a man who could be their father, uncle, or brother.

The idea that art's content is ultimately determined not only by its creator's intention but by all the possible interpretations and misinterpretations it prompts is basic to contemporary esthetics. In creating a work the artist initiates a collaboration with the public, and that collaboration is important because its self-revealing and catalytic nature adds to a greater understanding of the diverse components that form the work itself and its audience. Rather than presenting a fixed idea to a universal spectator, the artist sends out a coded proposition that will elicit reactions that illuminate the disparities between perception and expectation among those who respond.

By contrast, protest art tries to transmit the same message to all people, hoping to affirm in a uniform way the human values it proclaims. Piper's practice, however, follows the principle that the consciousness must be stimulated before the conscience can be addressed. Hence, the discomforts felt by the various people who entered her environment—anger at hearing the slurs; shame at having once uttered them; fear of showing true emotion; irritation

at being watched while trying to hide that emotion; awkwardness
in attempting to express empathy in a social vacuum; uncertainty
about whether to identify others with the man speaking; uncertainty
about identifying oneself with him; and uncertainty about being
identified with that man and, if so identified, in what way—all are
part of the raw material from which the work [*What It's Like, What
It Is #3*] is composed, and all bring to the surface the intricate, often
clashing patterns of feeling, thought, and behavior that make up the
irregular texture of race relations.

What It's Like, What It Is #3 is not designed solely to instruct or
provoke whites, but is a meticulously planned come-as-you-are-party
and, literally as well as figuratively, a place for reflection. It juxtaposes
the elegant otherworldliness of the art-space to the grim everyday
world inhabited by the man speaking. Instead of condemning the
former as "unreal" by interjecting the irrefutable reality of the latter,
and thereby reiterating the old radical argument that we cannot
afford artificial beauty until moral ugliness is defeated, Piper fuses
her dialectical opposites into a visual and spatial oxymoron. She thus
makes viewers conscious of the cognitive dissonance created by the
confrontation of the two forms of idealism she invoked—the dream of
esthetic harmony and the demand for social justice.

Incommensurable with one another, both of her symbolic terms
involve extremes of abstraction: the first, positive archetypes of
artistic perfection; the second, negative racial stereotypes. Although
the rational structures of the Minimalist architecture cannot be
reconciled with the irrational concepts at the heart of racism, in
context each compels our attention. The *relative* power of these two
concerns is decided largely by who we are and where we are. The
contemplation of absolutes—in which Piper, a Kantian philosopher,
firmly believes—requires a trust that the detachment required
will not be violated. Like other African Americans, Piper knows
by experience that access to the ivory tower is extremely limited
and that living in your head can be very risky. Nevertheless, by

evoking without irony exactly the sort of transcendence that has been a goal of art in every era, Piper asserts her equal claim to such transcendence—refusing, in effect, to cede her rights to the "White Cube" of high modernism simply because she is black, but also refusing to permit others to continue to enjoy its sanctuary without constant thought of what lies outside.

Piper's installation [at MoMA] therefore represented the opposite of what it was accused of being. Rather than merely taking sides and pointing fingers, the artist set out to demonstrate the complex uncertainties of interracial association by providing the grounds for a particularly intimate experience of ambivalence and alienation. Rather than casting aside art for the sake of a cause, Piper contrived a space of gleaming formality that plainly indicated her belief that esthetics are as much at stake in any critique of the existing order as social conditions are the inescapable framework of pure and practical reason.

Public Enemy (1991; **plates 18** and **19**), David Hammons's installation for *DIS*LOCATIONS, proceeded from an antithetical position. His project was inspired by the statue of Theodore Roosevelt that stands in front of New York's Museum of Natural History, which he passes frequently en route between uptown and downtown. Seated on horseback in a Gattamelata-like pose, the Imperial President and great outdoorsman is attended by two noble savages—one African, the other Native American. No longer willing to ignore or psychologically "grandfather" this glaringly anachronistic vision of the white man's burden, Hammons decided to symbolically unburden himself and the rest of New York of it.

The centerpiece of his environment was a precariously leaning three-dimensional photo-mural of the monument surrounded by sand bags, machine guns, patently fake sticks of dynamite, miniature cannons, and model attack planes zeroing in from above. Streamers and balloons festooned the ceiling in celebration of this domestic Desert Storm; deep piles of dried leaves covered the floor and filled the air with their fragrance. One full wall of floor-to-ceiling windows opened over the museum's garden; Hammons painted the other three walls a mottled sap green and scrolled them with gilt filigree so that they shaded into the gold-tinged autumnal trees outside. Combined with the leafy odor, the optical illusion made it feel as though one had stepped through the museum looking glass and back into the city. This blurring of the environmental boundaries was as basic to the work's meaning as its theatrically enhanced iconography. Hammons is an ironic poet of place, not an editorial cartoonist.

The city has long been Hammons preferred field of operations. For almost two decades, he has fashioned his major projects out of doors, from cast-off materials. In one piece, for instance, he attached basketball hoops and backboards to towering telephone poles, which he embellished with scavenged beer bottle caps, much as African craftsmen would decorate fetishes with cowry shells. In doing so, he created a monument to the lure and frustration that professional sports represent to young black men. Entitled *Higher Goals* (1986), these poles were planted in a vacant lot in Harlem and in a park in downtown Brooklyn, where those to whom they would have most meaning would easily run across them. Like much traditional African art—and like the costumes of Brooklyn's annual Caribbean Festival, which are part of that tradition's legacy in exile—Hammons's work is often inherently impermanent; in fact, none of these totems survive except in memory.

Nor does *Public Enemy* survive. What remains, besides a burlesque after-image of the tottering Rough-Rider and his carnival bright Armageddon, are some afterthoughts about the differences between it and Piper's piece. Although both dealt with race, they did so in ways that could hardly have been more dissimilar. In contrast to Piper's critical and esthetic restraint, Hammons used mordant but engaging humor coupled with a restless suspicion of institutional culture and its programmed audience ability to respond to what he calls the madness of

America. Altogether rejecting the "White Cube" as sterile and foreign, Hammons went beyond, introducing one discordant element into its precincts. He did everything he could to bring the street into the gallery—to turn the museum inside out and transform its marshaled public into meandering pedestrians.

From Piper and Hammons alone it is evident that among African-American artists who directly broach the matter in their work—and many do not—there is no single black view of racism. The assumption that Hammons and Piper were, in their separate ways, saying the same thing, begged the essential question of the relation of content to form, which is usually the first question asked of work dealing with less political issues but generally the last asked of art addressing controversial social problems. Rather than simply echoing each other's anger at a common enemy, Piper's and Hammons's installations revealed deeply considered and sharply contrasting attitudes toward the historical, philosophical, and artistic dimensions of their situation as black creators in a predominantly white society. Rather than constituting a chorus of accusations directed at the white majority, theirs was a dialogue between peers, conducted in the presence of that majority and serving as a forum for other "minorities" to join.

Many other voices are indeed taking part. While Piper, Hammons, and a handful of other artists whose careers began in the turmoil of the 1960s and early 1970s have re-emerged in recent years, we have also witnessed the rise of a younger generation of African-American painters, sculptors, photographers, multimedia artists, and critics. It is an artistic flowering that more than rivals the "Harlem Renaissance" of the 1920s and 1930s in its vigor, range of expression, and accomplishment. This new generation is very much aware of that past and of the episodic, often abruptly truncated development of previous movements and of the individual careers of those involved in them. The reason for such discontinuity is no mystery.

Attention to and inclusion of blacks in the established white art world is rarely timed to the creative seasons of the artists, but is all too often determined by the intermittent need of whites to check the pulse of the black community and publicly show their concern for it. Besides periodically reaffirming a moral involvement, this cyclical interest is prompted by an anxious desire to be told in encapsulated form what the current issues and etiquettes are so that one will know what to expect and how to behave. Once that desire has been satisfied, attention frequently wanders. The treatment awaiting black artists in these circumstances thus taps into the subtlest forms of bias, since it is predicated upon the notion that blacks are "the problem," and that among their number are those who, with the support of whites, will provide "the solution," or at least help keep matters from getting worse. It is in the spirit of tokenism, then, that African-American artists are first and foremost regarded as spokespersons of their kind. To avoid confusion, only so many can be given prominence at a time and only so long as their work clarifies rather than complicates the understanding that whites hope to gain of the prevailing state of interracial affairs.

In this context, the currently burgeoning and contentious community of black artists poses a special challenge to art institutions. The difficulty they must deal with, though few have fully accepted this fundamental reality, is not which black artists to select as representatives, but how to accommodate and present the multiplicity of esthetic attitudes and practices that demonstrably exist, and how, according to the other criteria, to integrate them into the broader history of art. Although focus-collections and alternative spaces have pioneered the way, the stage where it is acceptable to think of the work of black artists as merely tributary to the mainstream and therefore primarily suitable to the care of ethnically defined venues has long since passed. For the foreseeable future, however, these specialized institutions will continue to play the leading role in researching the past and nurturing new talent. They will always remain essential to the long-term support of African-American art in particular, just as the exclusively black colleges and universities have had and will have a special role in black education and cultural scholarship.

It is easy to compile a long and substantial roll of black visual artists, living and dead, whose work has in some measure contributed to the creation of a distinct and varied tradition, which is as much a part of the American tradition as a whole as the more generally acknowledged achievements in African-American literature, music, dance, and film. Among those who come to mind are Benny Andrews, Jean-Michel Basquiat, Romare Bearden, Dawoud Bey (**plate 20**), Robert Blackburn, Elizabeth Catlett (**plate 21**), Robert Colescott, Roy DeCarava, Beauford Delaney, David Driskell, Melvin Edwards, Sam Gilliam, Maren Hassinger, Richard Hunt, William H. Johnson, Jacob Lawrence, Norman Lewis, Al Loving, Tyrone Mitchell, Horace Pippin, Martin Puryear, Faith Ringgold (**plate 22**), Betye Saar, Alison Saar, Gary Simmons (**plate 27**), Lorna Simpson (**plate 28**), Clarissa Sligh, Alma Thomas, James Van Der Zee, and Carrie Mae Weems (**plates 23** and **24**), Charles White, Jack Whitten, William T. Williams, and Fred Wilson (**plates 25** and **26**).

Obviously, not all the serious creative work by black artists is of the first rank, just as not all the novels and essays by black authors worthy of being read are equally good. Nor is every Impressionist painting or Cubist sculpture that can be seen in our museums an undisputed masterpiece. Living culture is never just a matter of the widely agreed-upon greatness of a few artists or works. The best museums reflect this fact by showing and interrelating the various threads that give culture its textural richness. Given then that understanding depends on more than an appreciation of a handful of recognized classics, the sheer quantity and diversity of what is presently available necessitates comparative judgments of quality. True discernment—as opposed to gross discrimination, blanket approval, or the reflex preferences of unexamined taste—requires a general knowledge of the field that is constantly fed by ready access to and careful study of particular works. While established museums have made some progress by mounting retrospective exhibitions together with historical and contemporary surveys, chances for the general public, as well as for art professionals and patrons, to educate themselves are still few and far between. All too often these exhibitions are treated as socially mandated exercises, effectively signaling them as duties acquitted rather than as artistic options enthusiastically chosen. Moreover, the educational opportunity they create is frequently lost in the rush by the Right and the Left alike to use the art in question as interchangeable pawns in what has become a contest between a difference-muddling brand of liberalism and a difference-scorning school of conservatism.

Such was the case with the 1993 Whitney Biennial, which over the course of its rocky run became a virtual referendum on socially encoded art.[20] Having just defended two works in an exhibition that I organized against what I considered to be dismissive reviewers, I am not now going to venture a hit-and-run analysis of the flaws in the Whitney show, except to say that my disappointment with aspects of its conception and content was compounded by the unhappy realization that the backlash it had provoked was narrowing art-world appreciation of specific artists in whom I also shared an active interest.

Ironically, it was precisely because of its unevenness that the Biennial was the ideal occasion for setting standards for a variety of contemporary forms of "political" work. Disappointingly, few commentators took advantage of it. As with *DIS*LOCATIONS, almost none troubled themselves to describe in sufficient detail the appearance of the work or to ground their overall disapproval in any physically or visually verifiable specifics. In sum, these reviews constituted an inquest without evidence. That said, much of the work *was* limited by the obviousness of its confrontational attitude

20 Editor's note: the Whitney Biennial 1993 was curated by Thelma Golden, John G. Hanhardt, Lisa Phillips, and Elisabeth Sussman. It ran at the Whitney Museum of American Art, New York from 24 February to 20 June 1993.

or polemical intent. Felix Gonzalez-Torres, an artist represented in the previous Whitney Biennial but absent from this one, and one of the canniest young artists working with social signs in social settings, said it best: "Taken altogether, the show made it look as if we didn't know what metaphor was."[21]

There were notable exceptions. Some pieces with a specific point to make did so by indirect means. Byron Kim, a former student of figure painter Philip Pearlstein and a realist of the flesh in his own right, contributed a mural, *Synecdoche* (1991–92; **plate 29**), consisting of a grid of small rectangular paintings, each covered by a different monochrome coat of an earthen hue, ranging from bleached tan to rich coffee brown. At first sight, it looked like a tonal version of Ellsworth Kelly's 1951 chromatic grid, *Colors for a Large Wall*. Each panel of Kim's work was identified as the skin color of an individual. Finding sitters among strangers, friends, family, neighbors, and fellow artists, the artist would closely examine a patch of their skin before blending an assortment of paints to replicate its shade. Installed on the wall in alphabetical order, from left to right, according to the sitters' first names, the paintings evoked a sort of abstracted group portrait.

Just as Kelly observes color in the world around him, distills it and represents it in formal, sometimes chance-derived patterns that prepare one to experience the very same visual epiphanies as the painter, Kim, in assembling his modulated swatches, created a catalogue of nuances that, once noticed, trains the eye to recognize them in reality. In short, Kim's paintings provide the perfect optical tuning for a walk down Flatbush Avenue, or anywhere else in the city that one finds a broad range of human shades and tints. The simplicity of his premise guaranteed its effectiveness; like all successfully provocative works of art, Kim's prompted the viewer to experience a phenomenon before he made his case.

21 Felix Gonzalez-Torres, to the author in a public
    conversation at the Detroit Institute of Arts, winter 1993.

Glenn Ligon's multipanel installation, *Notes on the Margin of the Black Book* (1991–93; **plates 30** and **31**), also succeeded in opposing the assumption of uniformity with the reality of manifest variety. Ligon clipped the pages from Robert Mapplethorpe's 1986 album *The Black Book* bringing together a selection of his homoerotic photographs of nude African-American men, he framed them and arranged them in a two-tiered frieze on the wall, maintaining Mapplethorpe's original picture order. Between the rows of images, he placed small framed typed texts by diverse sources—including philosophers, activists, curators, historians, and religious evangelists. Some of these texts are written about Mapplethorpe's images, while others not. Together, they foreground the variety of interpretations on black masculinity in general and, specifically, the various fears and fantasies projected onto these pictures of black male nudes. Dispelling any notion that there exists a "politically correct" line toward the pictures and the highly charged mix of racial and sexual archetypes they directly or indirectly summon forth—the pagan, the buck, the blackamoor, the boy, the trick—these commentaries range from severe critique to elegiac anecdote. Almost paradigmatic of its type of Conceptual art, Ligon's work is demanding because it requires one to stand and read and piece together an understanding from the fragments provided. Its difficulty is not a form of esthetic punishment, but a necessarily taxing demonstration of how unexpected perceptions and spontaneous doubts emerge when one is confronted by images that have been deliberately reframed and separated from the "master" narratives that originally set the terms for their reception.

Or, to put it in plainer words, what if a gay black man should find himself attracted to depictions of other gay black men that were staged to suit the controlling fantasies of a white artist whose iconography flirts with racist stereotypes? This is essentially the problem Ligon set out to address; his work has so many meanings because his starting point was ambivalence, a heightened and authentic sensitivity to competing impulses and logical irreconcilable attitudes. Art of this kind cannot prove anything; it can only question belief by making believe, that is, by articulating all the unstated, incoherent, and often unacceptable thoughts and feelings that are triggered by the experiences and signs that connect us to the social realm. To have any value to the maker, and to therefore be convincing to the public that is called upon to trust and identify with the artist's speculations and projections, such work must begin with the unexamined and the undecided, and must be content to remain there. All we can expect is increased clarity about matters of great import but also great convulsion.

It is far more important to explore our own involvement in the errors and evils of any existing social or ideological order than it is to assign blame. Bad political art trades in pure guilt and pure virtue. Looking back on *DIS*LOCATIONS (1991–92), the 1993 Whitney Biennial, all the recent exhibitions that have raised similar issues, and yet further back in the long history of social commitment in modern art—a heritage one may trace on the walls of MoMA, from the overt symbolism of Russian Constructivism, German Dada, Italian Futurism, and Mexican muralism to the political undertones of Pop, Minimalism, and Conceptualism—it is obvious that the lessons to be learned are embedded in unresolved contradictions intrinsic to the work and the condition in which it was produced. Conservatives with perfect hindsight ridicule the failed dreams of the past; those more forward-looking study them for the symptoms of self-deception. Mindful of those failed dreams, the leading figures in the current generation of politically inclined artists are practicing skeptics.

The moral high ground has been cut out from under us on all sides. Art made for naively altruistic or therapeutic purposes is no longer plausible. On that score the Right is right. It is no longer possible to speak for others, or to presume to fight their causes, when it is obvious that we have lost the ability to speak honestly for ourselves and cannot fully comprehend how our fate is connected to theirs. The problem is to find a way to live in an America that cannot live with itself: to proceed as if the American model of democratic pluralism worked or could be made to work even when all around us its juridical and economic promises are being broken or indefinitely postponed and its cultural and ethnic make-up undergoes perpetual transformation. To define one's position in that setting one must accept, if not embrace, change and instability; one must be ready on an ongoing basis to renegotiate the social contract that binds each to all.

Balkanization is the reactionary aspect of the multiculturalist response to that challenge. In heterogeneous societies, the tendency toward fragmentation rather than consolidation is profound, recurring, and potentially disastrous—witness the ruinous resumption of ancient conflicts in the European region that gives us the term. Lynching, riots, gang-banging, and vigilante action prove that ethnic turf wars in the United States can be every bit as violent, although here the problem is primarily the formation of social cysts. Though no one, save the decimated Native American population, can claim a primordial homeland, territory and allegiance are plainly marked by speech, dress, diet, music, and other symbols of group affinity.

Fastening on an essentialist idea of the individual and the community, those tempted to confine themselves to voluntary ghettos must eventually contend with latent doubts and insecurities that mutate and fester in isolation, jeopardizing survival as surely as does the harassment of outsiders. Under these circumstances, denial gradually undermines affirmation, and idealized self-images threaten to become self-caricatures equal to the hostile representations advanced by the larger culture surrounding the smaller enclave. The most effective critics of such regression are among those who have felt its attraction but, rejecting outward trappings, have learned to assert and protect themselves with less literal or constricting means. On this, I turn to James Baldwin, as quoted by Glenn Ligon in another recent art project, *Good Mirrors Are Not Cheap* (1992):

*Identity would seem to be a garment with which one covers
the nakedness of the self: in which case, it is best that
the garment be loose, a little like the robes of the desert,
through which robes one's nakedness can always be felt,
and sometimes discerned. This trust in one's nakedness is
all that gives one the power to change one's robes.*[22]

Another black artist already discussed, David Hammons, is just such a nomad, and his fierce vulnerability is the mark of his freedom. Like Baldwin, moreover, Hammons constantly reminds the public of his status as an outsider to Western Culture, while simultaneously sampling it at will. The liberty he claims is a license to use whatever he wants while ignoring whatever is unrelated to the formulation of an alternative African-American world view. In the tradition of jazz composer Sun Ra's black science-fiction utopia—which combined triple-whammy minstrel comedy, radical musical invention, and ardent cultural nationalism—Hammons wants it all, and will use anything. With Sun Ra at his back, he draws Federico Fellini to his side, reversing the canonical progression of influences by Africanizing European models—in this case, Fellini's baroque recasting of the modernist absurd.

The selective assimilation of foreign ideas does not under these conditions entail the wholesale social assimilation of the person involved. Quite the opposite, the process begins and ends with an acute sense of separateness. That artists such as Hammons insist on that separateness is not a denial of the debt, but a refusal to play the colonial to a culture that is theirs only through historical imposition and individual curiosity and acquisition. Anyone who is scandalized by recent critiques of Eurocentrism and thinks that they are symptomatic of an unprecedented and wholesale denigration of Western tradition, should first consider the

22 James Baldwin quoted by Glenn Ligon in his installation *Good Mirrors Are Not Cheap,* Whitney Museum of American Art, New York (17 July – 28 November 1992).

following remarks by Baldwin, written in 1955, when he lived as an expatriate in a Swiss village:

> *I know, in any case, that the most crucial time in my own development came when I was forced to recognize that I was a kind of bastard of the West: when I followed the line of my past, I did not find myself in Europe but in Africa. And this meant in some subtle way, in a really profound way, I brought to Shakespeare, Bach, Rembrandt, and to the stones of Paris, to the Cathedral of Chartres and to the Empire State Building a special attitude. These are not really my creations, they did not contain my history: I might search in vain forever for any reflection of myself. I was an interloper: this was not my heritage.*[23]

Nevertheless, he added, "The cathedral at Chartres ... says something to the people of this village which it cannot say to me; but it is important to understand that this cathedral says something to me which it cannot say to them."[24] That statement, and the efforts of Hammons, Piper, Ligon, and many other black artists active at the moment demonstrates the possibility of remaking and reinterpreting the creations of the West in light of that "special attitude."

Commuting between New York and Rome, Hammons is currently the most remarkable agent and symbol of this cross-fertilization. African-American critics, whose number has steadily grown over the last decade and whose works are featured with growing frequency in glossy as well as alternative journals, are seizing the same opportunity. Hilton Als, bell hooks, Kellie Jones, Lisa Jones, Calvin Reid, Greg Tate, and Michelle Wallace head the list of such younger writers and all approach the visual arts as cultural critics in the broadest sense. In talking back to power, language is transformed. Saluting and

---

23 James Baldwin, *Notes of a Native Son* (Bantam Books, New York, 1964), p.4.

24 Ibid., p.147.

amending Baldwin, writer Greg Tate's collected essays are entitled *Flyboy in the Buttermilk* (1992), and in them post-structuralist thinking picks up an urban American slant and a hip-hop beat, which ironically restores to it the kind of antic wordplay generally lost in the translation from allusive French to academic English.[25] If this new generation of writers and artists continues to concentrate on defining themselves in terms of the immediate ambiguities and tensions they face daily, remember this also from Baldwin:

> *I have not written about being a Negro at such length because I do not expect that to be my only subject, but only because it was the gate I had to unlock before I could hope to write about anything else.*[26]

Well before Baldwin, the works originating from this imperative already constituted one of the major chapters of American literature. Looking back, but also at the present, one can see an equally rich contribution to modernism in the visual arts. For mainstream institutions to miss out on this because of political pressures, or because of initially unsuccessful attempts at coping with disparate material and a diverse public, would constitute an abdication of their fundamental esthetic responsibility as well as of their civic role. Above all, it is for the sake of their primary obligation to artistic seriousness that such institutions must pay attention to these developments. Any claim to representing the art of our time that neglects mention of them is fraudulent. Continual support of black artists is of the essence; informed respect is not a sometime thing. The crucial test, therefore, is not one of vague intentions but whether such institutions are honest enough in their purpose to make such work an integral, rather than an incidental, part of their program, and strong enough in their conviction to withstand the stress that such inclusiveness will inevitably put upon them.

25 Baldwin's essay, "A Fly in Buttermilk," appears in *Nobody Knows My Name: More* *Notes of a Native Son* (Dell, New York, 1961).

26 Ibid., p.5.

The current stand-off between those who want to open museums to new art and new audiences and those determined to turn them into fortified churches hinges on this question. At the heart of the matter lies a crucial irony: the most ardent partisans of cultural protectionism are those with the least faith in the vitality of the heritage they defend. Although Neo-Conservatives hoping to keep pluralism in check trumpet the superiority of what they selectively call "Western" civilization, they ignore its deep indebtedness to other cultures and show their basic lack of confidence in its capacity to assimilate further outside influences. Their "West" is a neurasthenic invalid protesting its faith in a quack regimen, all the while ignoring that its superstitions will hasten, not halt, its decline.

Such reactionaries see themselves as valiant guardians of high culture against low culture, eternal values against ephemeral fashions. Their mantra is English critic Matthew Arnold's vow to be "bound by my own definition of criticism: a disinterested endeavor to learn and propagate the best that is known and thought in the world." It is a noble premise. Alfred H. Barr, Jr., for one, certainly felt something akin to this ambition. But his expansive idea of where the best might be found and his belief that identifying it was a matter of trial and error qualify the abstract simplicity of Arnold's credo. Moreover, Barr realized that the best is not so easily swamped by the lesser, though we may be unprepared to recognize it at first sight or even after the passage of years. Art is mysterious. Like other mysteries, it is a puzzle before it becomes meaningful; something obscure before it becomes clear. And still, there remains the possibility that we have misunderstood. A work's significance is always a matter of contention, and thus the canon of greatness is inherently subject to challenge and reappraisal. It is the exercise of critical intelligence that keeps art fresh, and freshness, as American critic Harold Rosenberg once said, is the mark of quality in modernism.

Unwilling to enter into the fray, as Barr did, the advocates of the static view of culture fancy themselves kindred souls to Arnold's poetic protagonist, watching from afar as "ignorant armies clash by night." In reality, they are responsible for inciting many of the conflicts they deplore. Despite their refrain that politics and art have nothing to do with one another, their obsession with power belies their disinterestedness and their refusal to take responsibility for politicizing esthetic discussion is just one example of their dishonesty. Hoping to further distract attention from their activism while damning that of their adversaries, Neo-Conservatives are prone to reciting W. H. Auden's dictum that "poetry makes nothing happen." Disillusioned with the romantic radicalism he espoused in the 1930s, Auden was renouncing the hope that poetry could make men good or at least arouse them against evil. But those who most regularly invoke this line as criticism of contemporary art and literature are agents of a well-schooled anti-intellectualism for which Auden should not be blamed. Devaluing the life of the mind while pretending to honor it, they argue that esthetic thought and feeling have no bearing on other types of experience, and the proportion and disturbances of art offer no useful insights into the structure of reality.

Although "poetry" cannot ensure any actual result, art in all forms makes the world imaginable. To the extent that America has lost the ability to picture itself whole and in all its dimensions and thus to freely speculate on how these many aspects affect and fuse with one another, it has lost its way and risks forfeiting its patrimony and its prospects. In this of all societies, a sense of social momentum and cultural cohesion depends on collective involvement in the constant revision of our collective self-image. America has never been a fixed entity; it is a process. By virtue of its perpetually unfinished becoming, it remains the most modern of states. Implicit in our history and our institutions as well as in our art is the realization that form without formation is impossible, and that growth necessarily admits and often thrives on mutations and admixtures.

No artist in our past understood this better or expressed it with more fervent and fully tempered optimism than poet Walt Whitman (**plate 32**). America's great migrations flowed into his poetry, and his prose recorded its fratricidal Civil War. A man of easy acquaintance and immense appetite, Whitman was ready-made for the flux of his era. His gifts of concentration allowed him to transform hard quotidian fact into a pulsing cosmology. His distinction was in noticing and embracing distinctions. Antitheses and antagonisms did not trouble him, but instead spurred his desire to find a common ground. Singing himself and others, he sang the unity of opposites.

If any part of our cultural heritage has been overlooked or taken for granted in recent years, it is the one Whitman personifies. And if our desire to reconnect past and present is sincere, it is there we should start. Gazing through his prism out over democratic vistas, the view has changed but not diminished. The echoed speech of his fellow citizens that he transmitted to us over space and time still rings true, but differently as his own voice has dissolved into a chorus. Men and women like those whom Whitman met and celebrated, now celebrate themselves. The questions he asked them, they ask each other and answer in their own name. They in our day, as much as he in his, value variety and see themselves as individuals in a multitude. More than a descant to his national hymn, their cumulative sound is its fully orchestrated continuation. Whatever dissonance one hears was always there. Its amplified intensities and their relation to overall harmony are the inevitable and enriching consequence of additional and unique timbres.

Riding on the subway between my home in Flatbush and my job at The Museum of Modern Art, I often thumbed through *Leaves of Grass* (1855). Gently hypnotized by the sway of the train and the cadences of Whitman's verse, I sometimes felt an invisible surge of energy in the crammed-together bodies and the blank or wary, mostly black, faces. And I would sense a kind of bond that nothing in their outward demeanor demonstrated, which made me wonder if only a catastrophe could bring that vigor and connectedness to the surface, or if some other cause, some word, look, or act of recognition might reveal it. I have had the same sensation reading Langston Hughes (**plate 33**), Allen Ginsberg (**plate 34**), and Gwendolyn Brooks (**plate 35**). When this feeling came over me I waited for an overt confirmation of my intuition, all the while knowing how unlikely that was. I keep waiting. Because I also know that between a rock and a hard place there is always space for the imagination. If we cannot escape our predicament, we must live our lives and dream our dreams in the gaps we find and in the time allotted us. It is only reasonable to think that others nearby know this too, and that from any one of them might come the pall-breaking sign. Wherever it appears, we cannot afford to miss it.

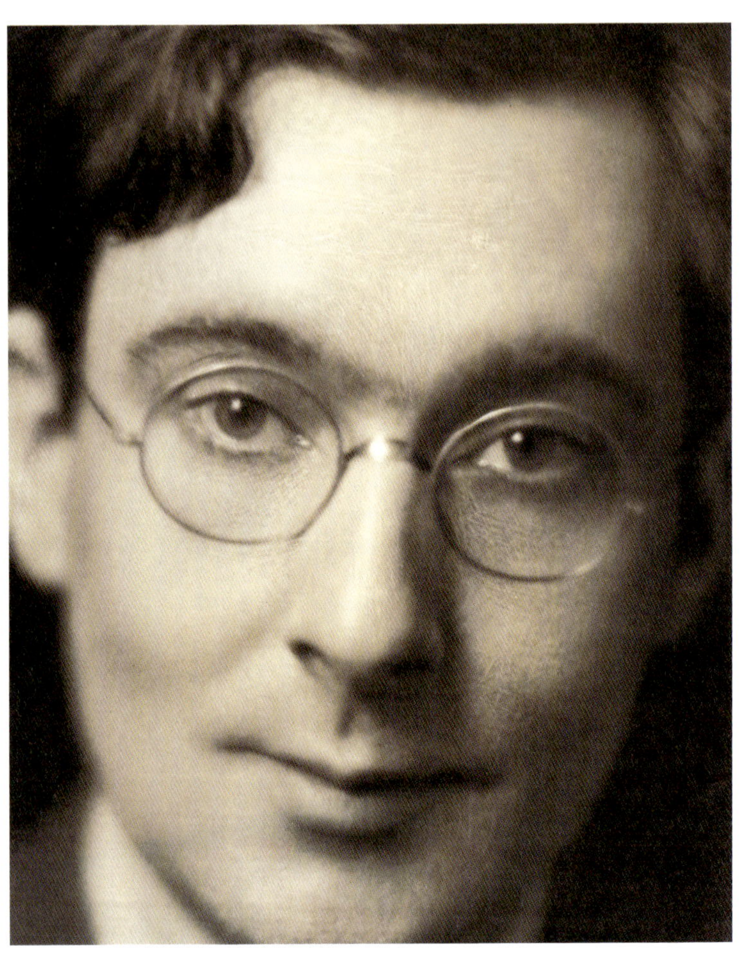

1

Photograph of Alfred H. Barr, Jr., 1929

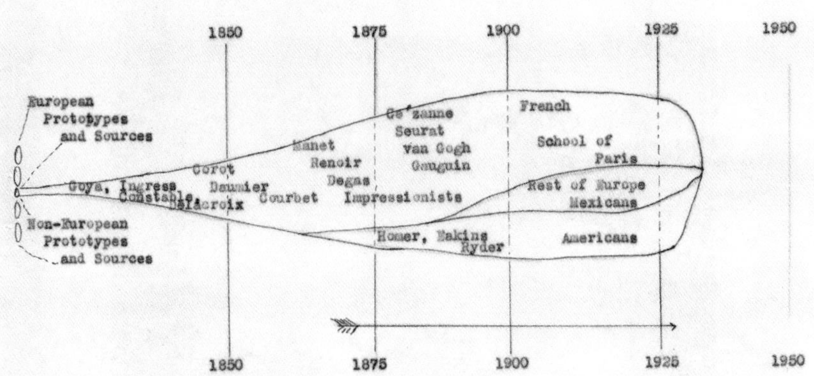

2

Alfred H. Barr, Jr., "Torpedo" diagram of the ideal permanent collection of The Museum of Modern Art, New York as advanced in 1933. Offset, printed in black, 20.3 × 29.2 cm (8 ½ × 11 in.)

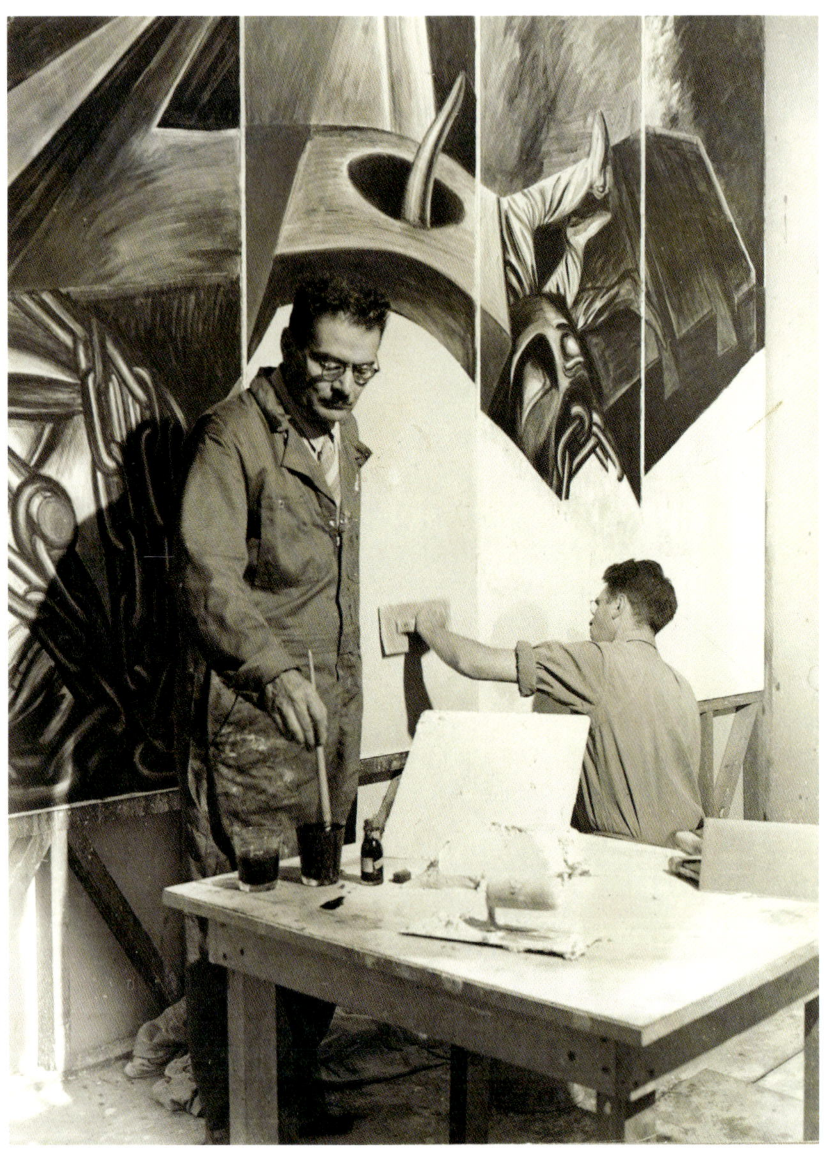

3

José Clemente Orozco with his assistant Lewis Rubenstein at work
on his fresco *Dive Bomber and Tank* at The Museum of Modern
Art, New York in June 1940 for the exhibition *Twenty Centuries
of Mexican Art*, MoMA, New York (15 May – 30 September 1940)

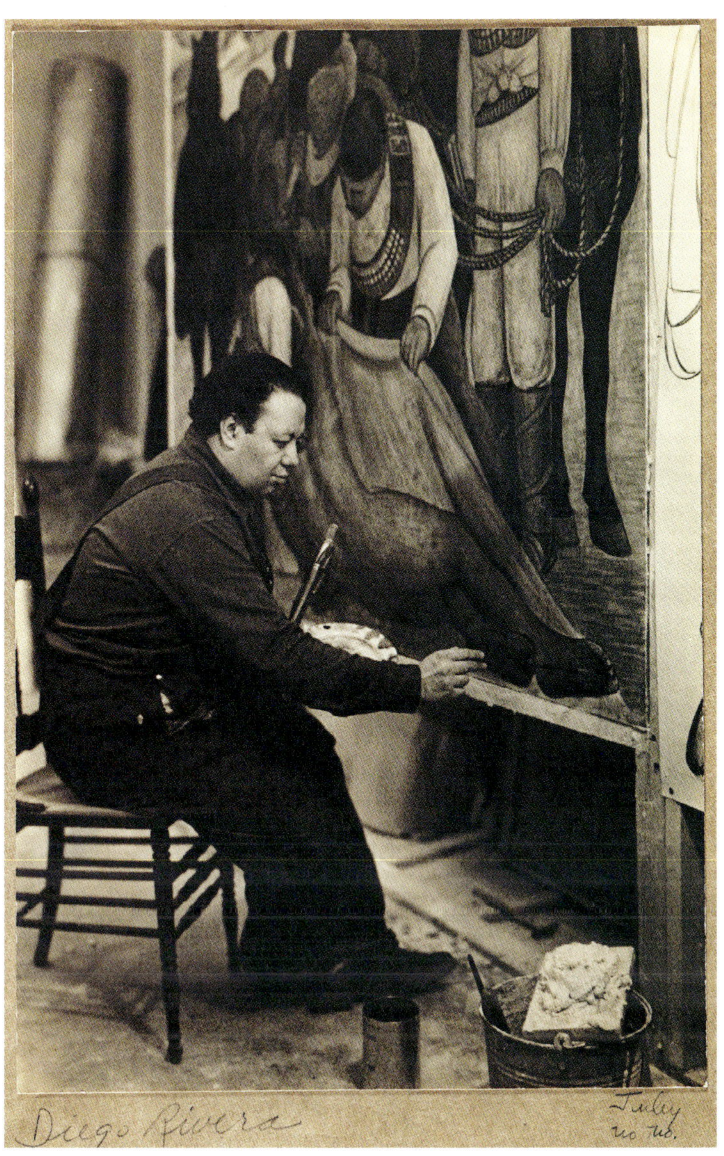

4

Diego Rivera painting *Liberation of the Peon* in
1931 at The Museum of Modern Art, New York for
inclusion in the exhibition *Diego Rivera*, MoMA,
New York (22 December 1931 – 27 January 1932)

The Museum of Modern Art Archives, New York. Digital image
© 2024 The Museum of Modern Art, New York / Scala, Florence

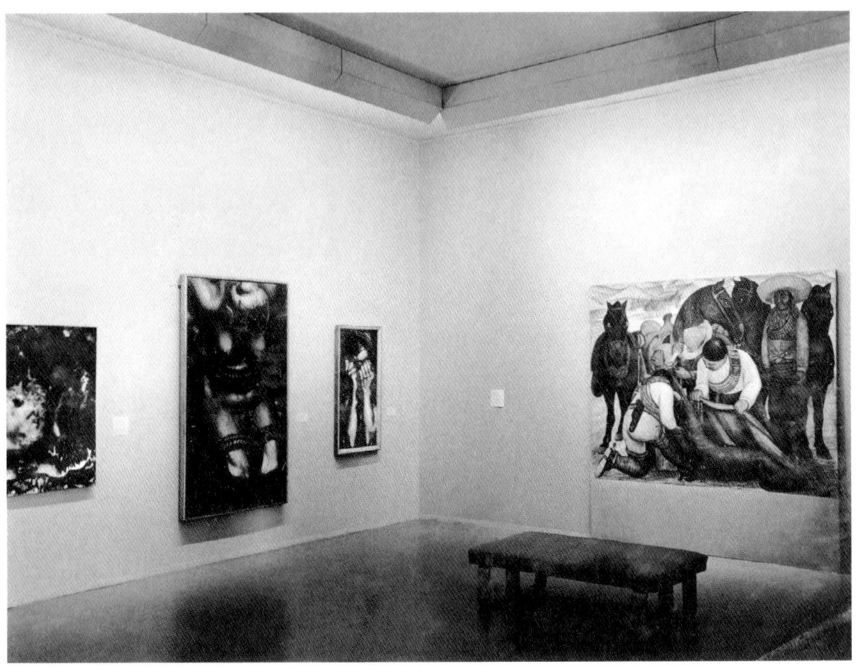

5
Installation view of the exhibition *Twenty Centuries
of Mexican Art*, The Museum of Modern Art, New
York (15 May – 30 September 1940). On the far
right is Diego Rivera's *Liberation of the Peon* (1931)

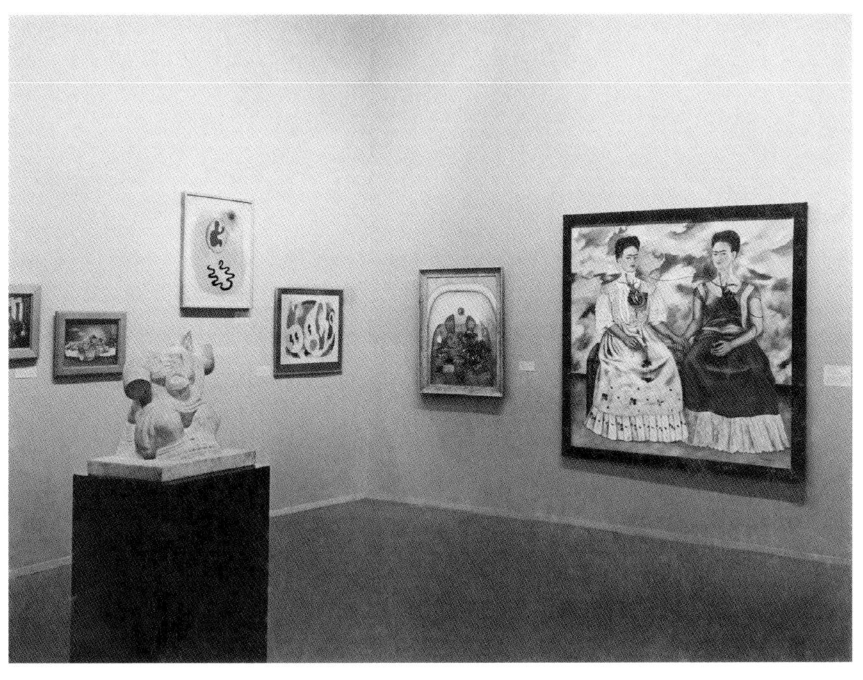

6
Installation view of the exhibition *Twenty Centuries of Mexican Art*, The Museum of Modern Art, New York (15 May – 30 September 1940)

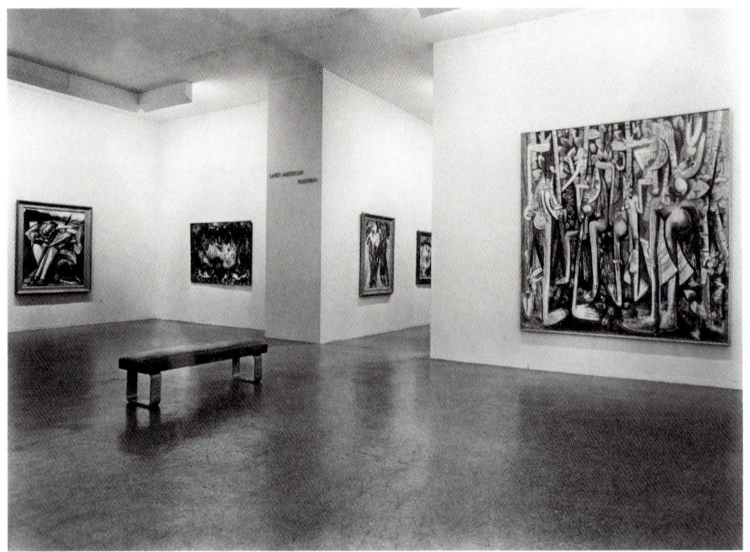

7
Installation view of the exhibition *Recent Acquisitions*, The
Museum of Modern Art, New York (25 July – 5 November 1950)
showing Wifredo Lam's 1943 *The Jungle* (far right) and David
Alfaro Siqueiros's 1936 *Collective Suicide* (second from left)

Wifredo Lam Artwork © ADAGP, Paris and DACS, London 2024.
David Alfaro Siqueiros Artwork © DACS 2024. Photo: Soichi Sunami.
The Museum of Modern Art Archives, New York. Digital image
© 2024 The Museum of Modern Art, New York / Scala, Florence

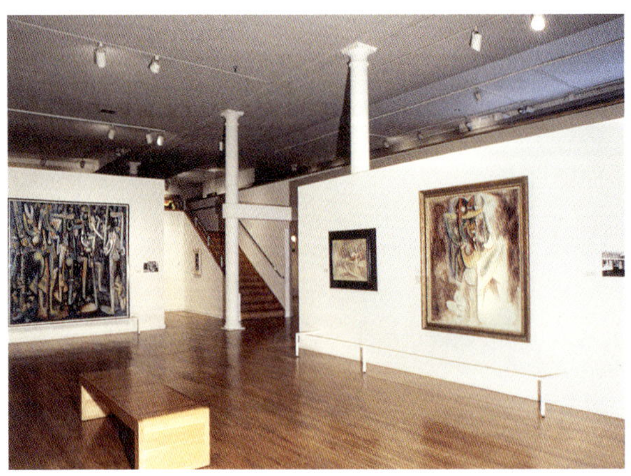

8
Installation view of
*Wifredo Lam and
His Contemporaries,
1938–1952*, Studio
Museum in Harlem
(6 December 1992 – 11
April 1993). On the far
left is Wifredo Lam's
The Jungle (1943)

Courtesy The Studio
Museum in Harlem
Archives. Wifredo Lam
Artwork © ADAGP, Paris
and DACS, London 2024

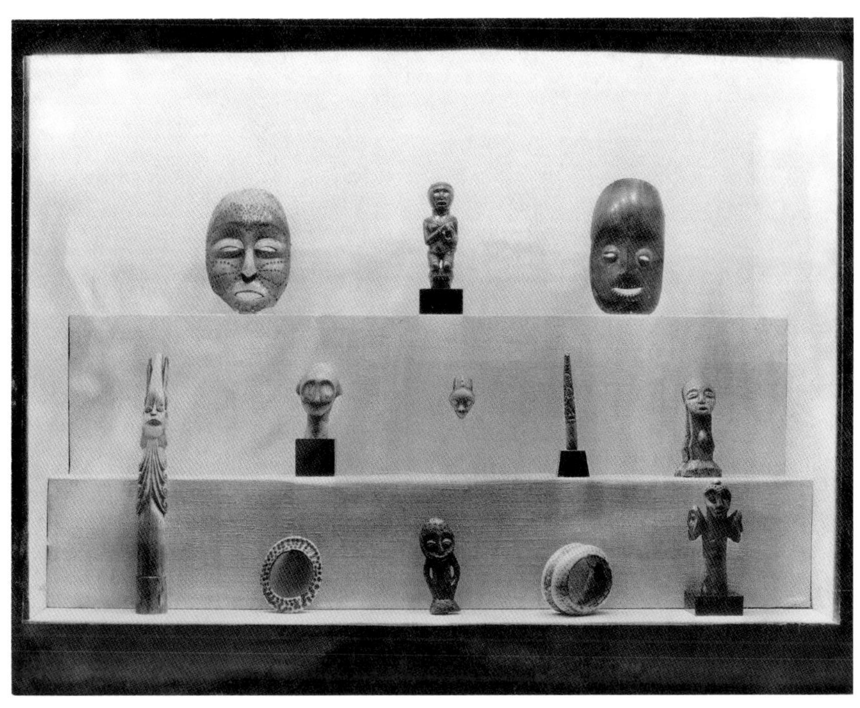

9

Installation view of the exhibition *African Negro Art*, The Museum of Modern Art, New York (18 March – 19 May 1935)

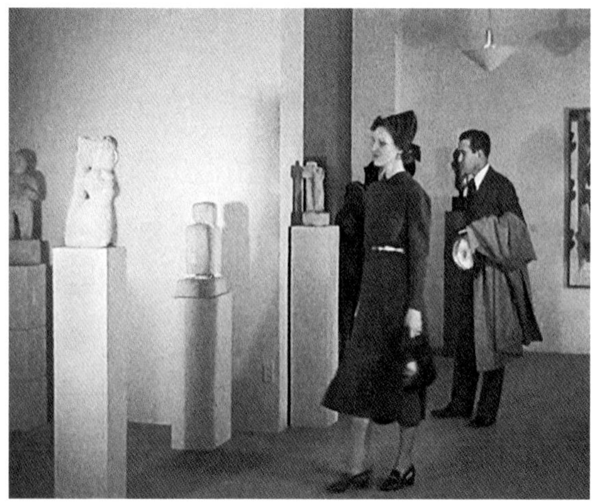

10

Installation view of the exhibition *Sculpture by William Edmondson*, The Museum of Modern Art, New York, 1937. Still from the film *New York*, 1937 (black-and-white, silent, 46 sec.)

British Pathé Archives

11

William Edmondson at work, still from the film *New York*, 1937 (black-and-white, silent, 46 sec.) devoted to the 1937 exhibition *Sculpture by William Edmondson* at The Museum of Modern Art, New York

British Pathé Archives

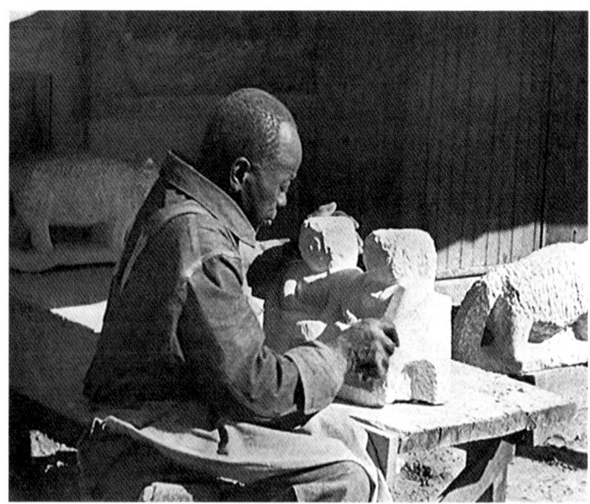

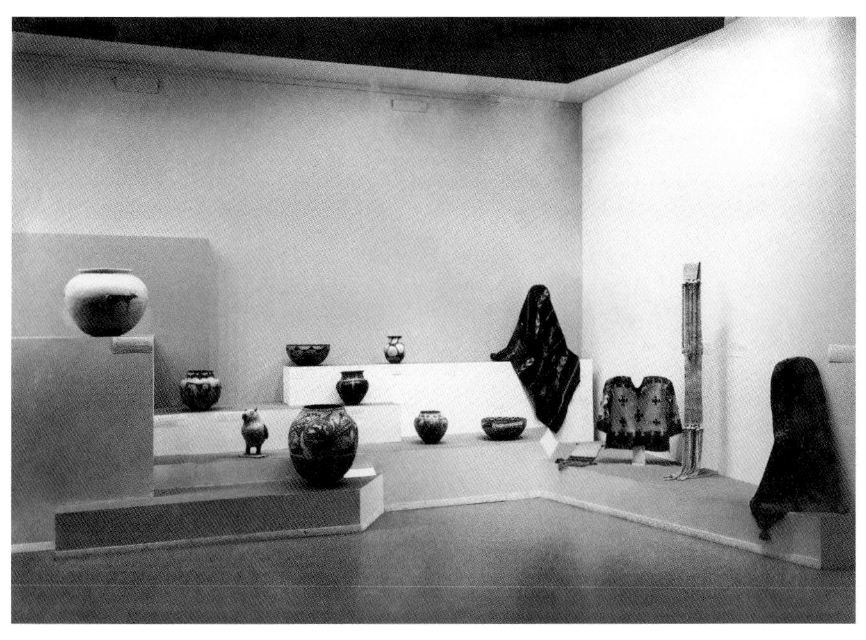

12
Installation view of the exhibition *Indian Art
of the United States*, The Museum of Modern
Art, New York (22 January – 27 April 1941)

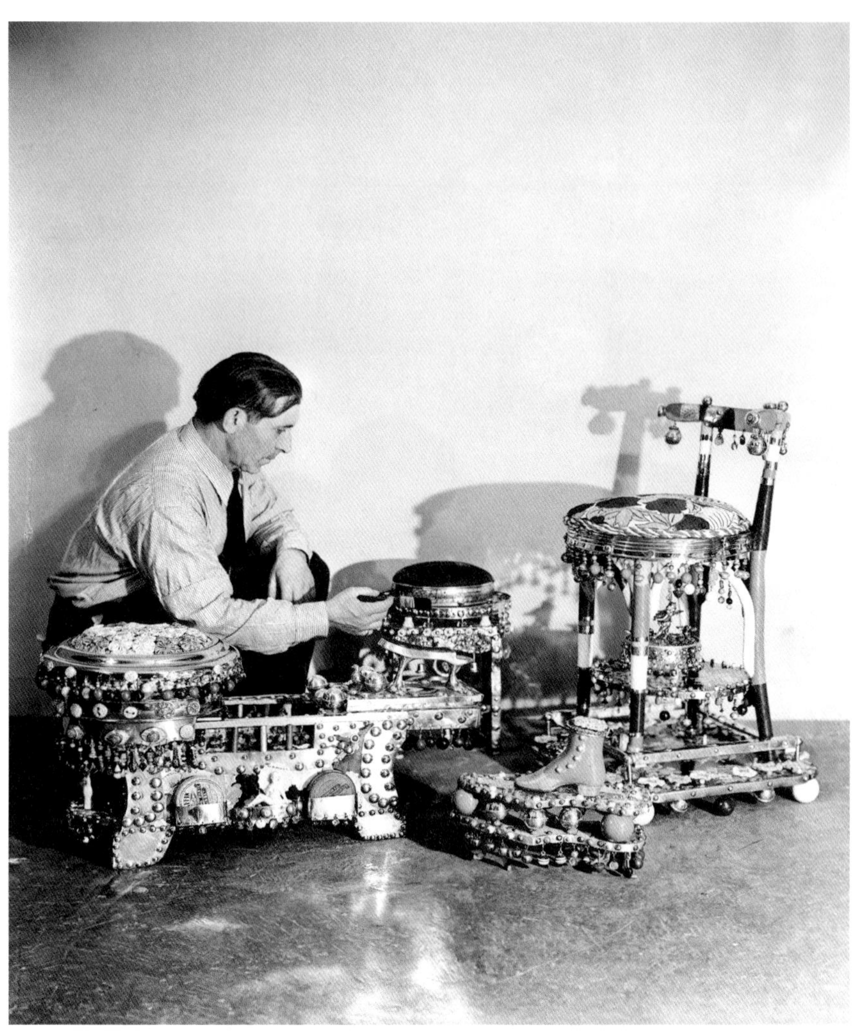

13
Joe Milone and his shoeshine equipment
in the exhibition *Joe Milone's Shoe Shine
Stand*, The Museum of Modern Art, New
York (22 December 1942 – 10 January 1943)

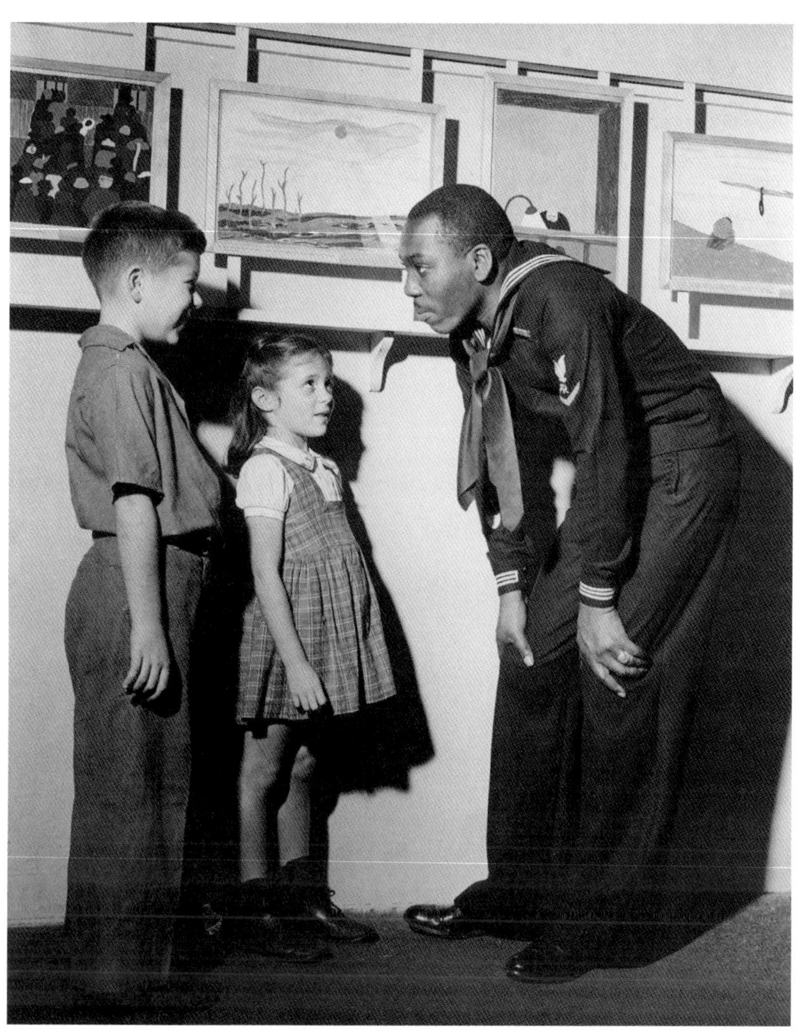

14
Jacob Lawrence shown with David and Margaret
Charney at the preview of his exhibition *Paintings
by Jacob Lawrence*, The Museum of Modern Art,
New York (10 October – 5 November 1944)

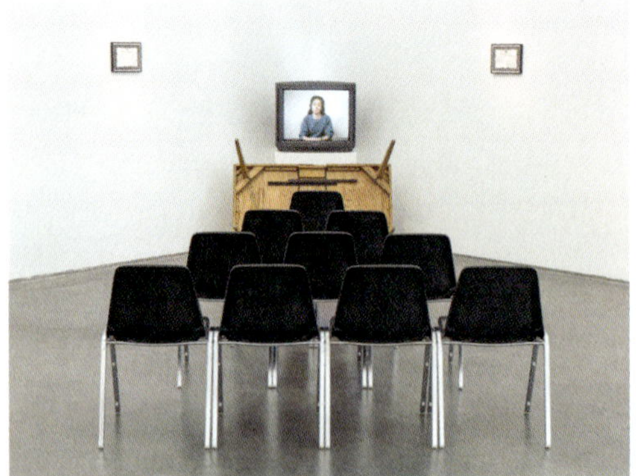

15
Adrian Piper
Cornered, 1988
Video (color, sound), 17 min.,
with monitor, table, chairs,
and two framed birth
certificates of Adrian Piper's
father Daniel R. Piper,
dimensions variable

Museum of Contemporary Art, Chicago.
Bernice and Kenneth Newberger Fund.
© Adrian Piper Research Archive
(APRA) Foundation Berlin. Photo:
Nathan Keay / MCA Chicago

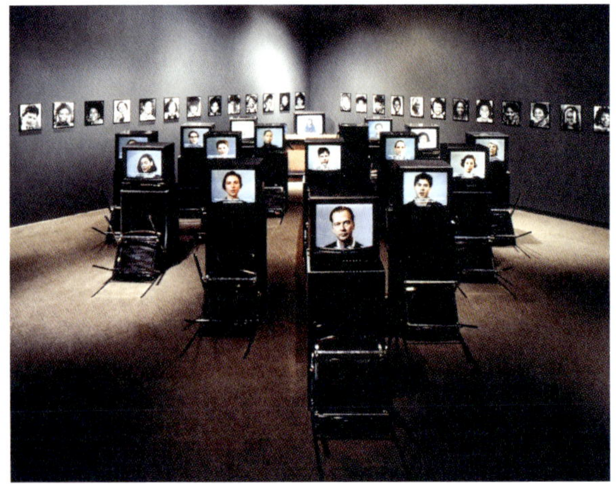

16
Adrian Piper
Out of the Corner, 1990
Seventeen-channel video installation (color, sound) 26 min.,
with seventeen monitors, sixteen pedestals, table, twenty-three
chairs, and sixty-four gelatin silver prints, dimensions variable

Whitney Museum of American Art, New York. Gift of the Peter Norton Family
Foundation. © Adrian Piper Research Archive (APRA) Foundation Berlin

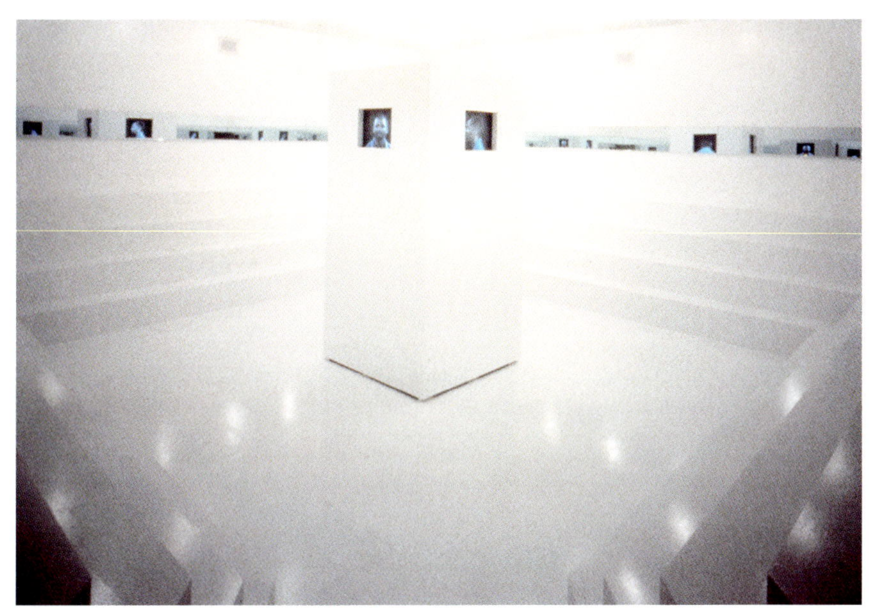

17
Adrian Piper
What It's Like, What It Is #3, 1991
Video installation. Video (color, sound),
constructed wood environment, four monitors,
mirrors, and lighting, dimensions variable

The Museum of Modern Art, New York. Acquired in part
through the generosity of Lonti Ebers, Marie-Josée and Henry
Kravis, Candace King Weir, Lévy Gorvy Gallery, and with
support from The Modern Women's Fund. Installation view
from the exhibition *DIS*LOCATIONS, The Museum of Modern
Art, New York (20 October 1991 – 7 January 1992). © Adrian
Piper Research Archive (APRA) Foundation Berlin. Photo: Scott
Frances / Esto, courtesy The Museum of Modern Art, New York

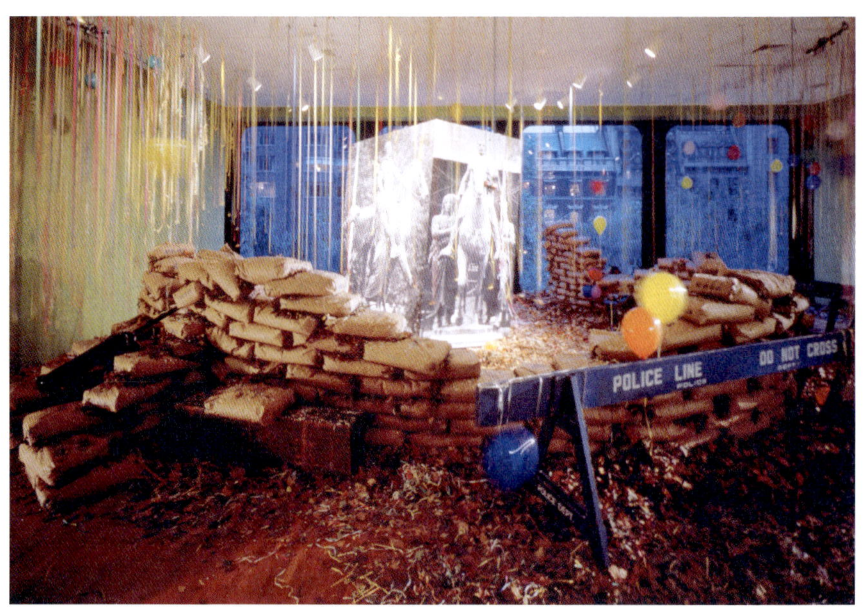

18

Installation view of *Public Enemy* (1991; no longer
extant) by David Hammons, from the exhibition
*DIS*LOCATIONS, The Museum of Modern Art,
New York (20 October 1991 – 7 January 1992)

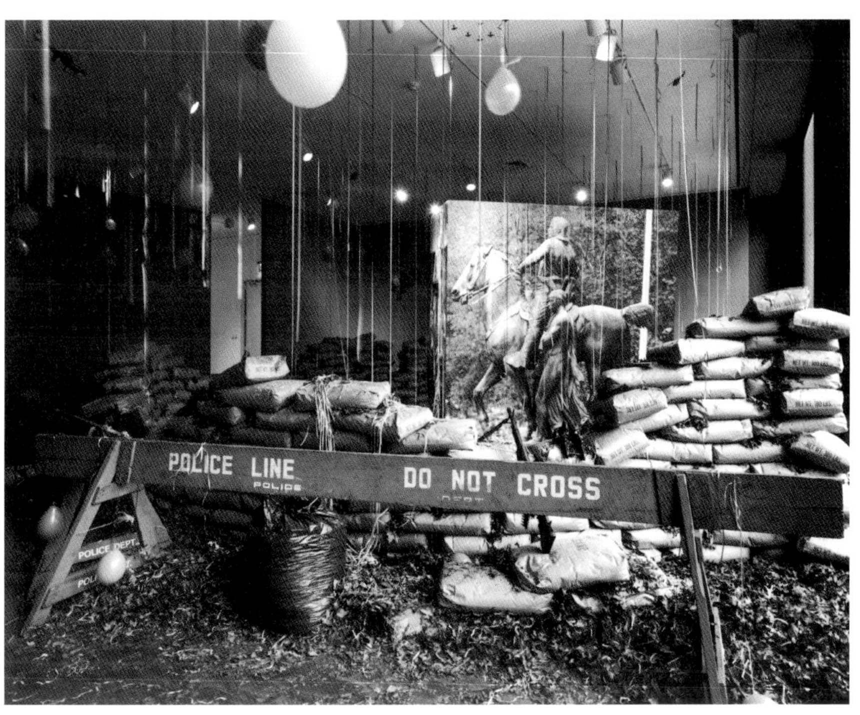

19
Installation view of *Public Enemy* (1991; no longer
extant) by David Hammons, from the exhibition
*DIS*LOCATIONS, The Museum of Modern Art,
New York (20 October 1991 – 7 January 1992)

The Museum of Modern Art Archives, New York.
© David Hammons. Digital image © 2024 The
Museum of Modern Art, New York / Scala, Florence

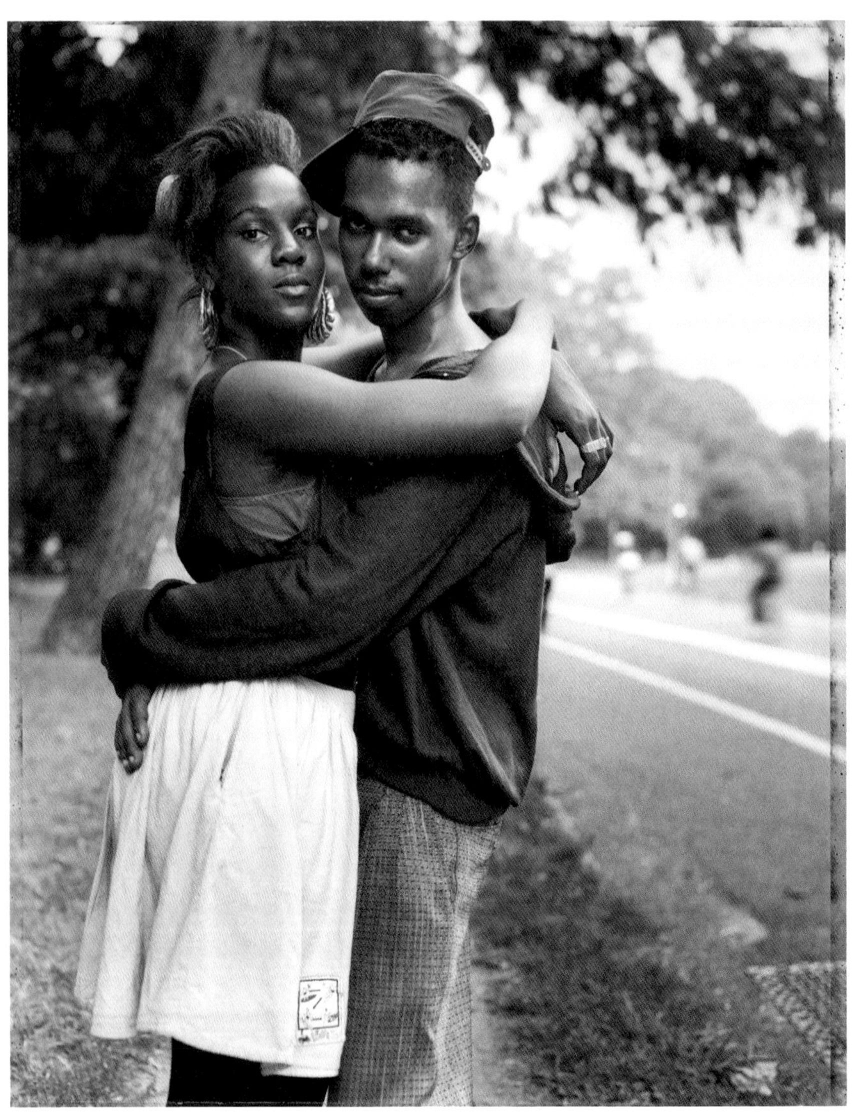

20
Dawoud Bey
A Couple in Prospect Park, Brooklyn, N.Y., 1990
Archival pigment photograph,
101.6 × 76.2 cm (40 × 30 in.)

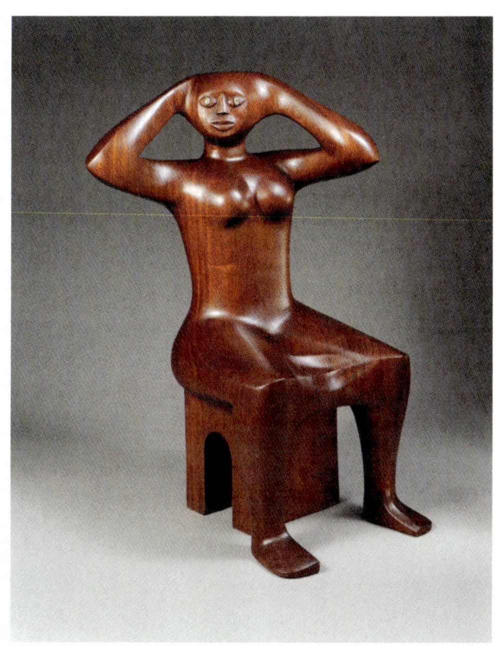

21
Elizabeth Catlett
Woman Fixing Her Hair, 1993
Mahogany and opals, 68.6 ×
45.7 × 33 cm (27 × 18 × 13 in.)

The Metropolitan Museum of Art,
Hortense and William A. Mohr
Sculpture Purchase Fund, 1993.
© Catlett Mora Family Trust / VAGA
at Artists Rights Society (ARS), N.Y.
and DACS, London 2024. Image ©
The Metropolitan Museum of Art / Art
Resource / Scala, Florence

22
Faith Ringgold
Picasso's Studio, 1991
Acrylic on canvas;
printed and tie-dyed
fabric, overall: 185.4 ×
172.7 cm (73 × 68 in.)

Worcester Art Museum,
Charlotte E. W. Buffington
Fund. © 2024 Faith
Ringgold / Artists Rights
Society (ARS), New
York and DACS, London.
Courtesy ACA Galleries,
New York. Photo ©
Worcester Art Museum /
Charlotte E. W. Buffington
Fund / Bridgeman Images

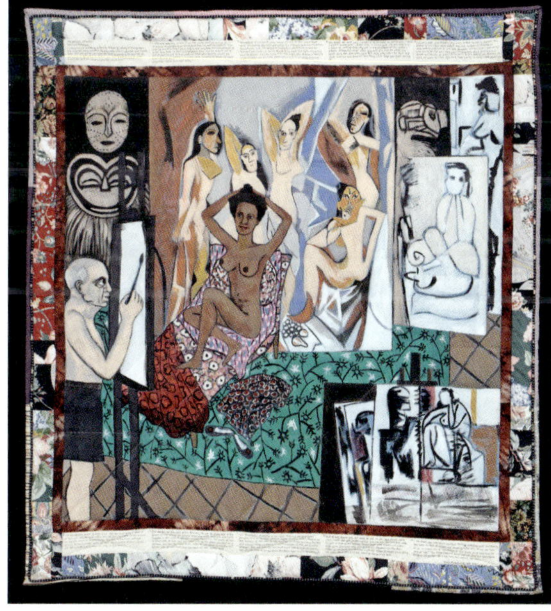

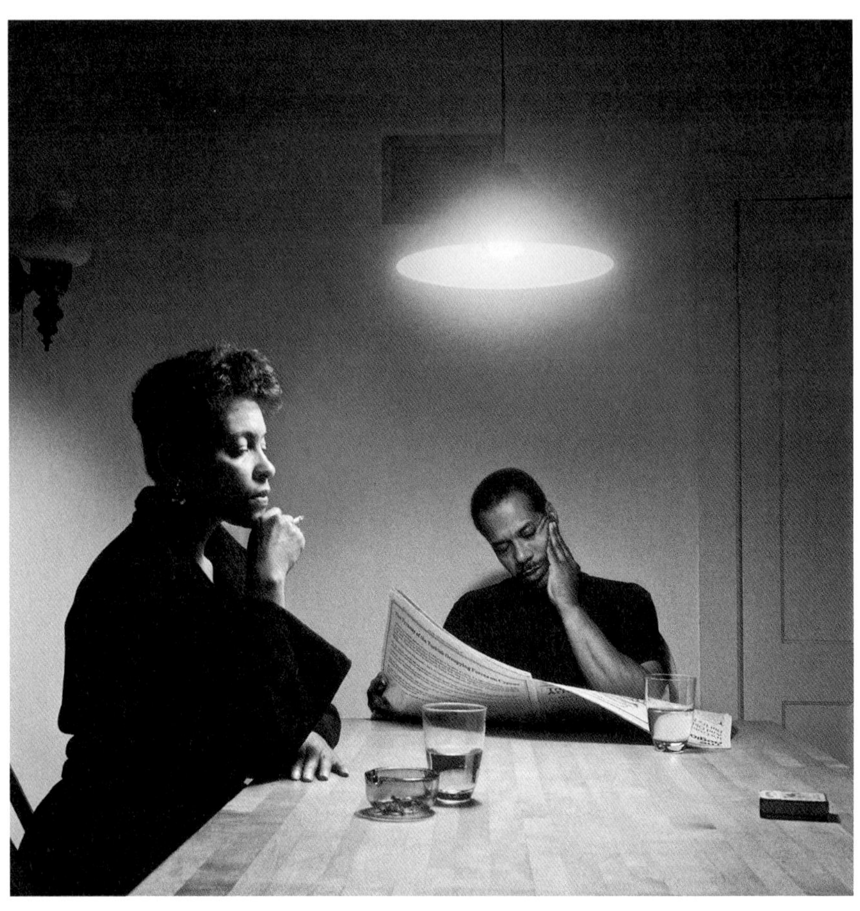

23
Carrie Mae Weems
Untitled (Man reading Newspaper), 1990
Gelatin silver print, 69.1 × 69.1 cm (27 ³⁄₁₆ × 27 ³⁄₁₆ in.)

Courtesy the artist and Jack Shainman Gallery,
New York, Galerie Barbara Thumm, Berlin, and
Fraenkel Gallery, San Francisco. © Carrie Mae Weems

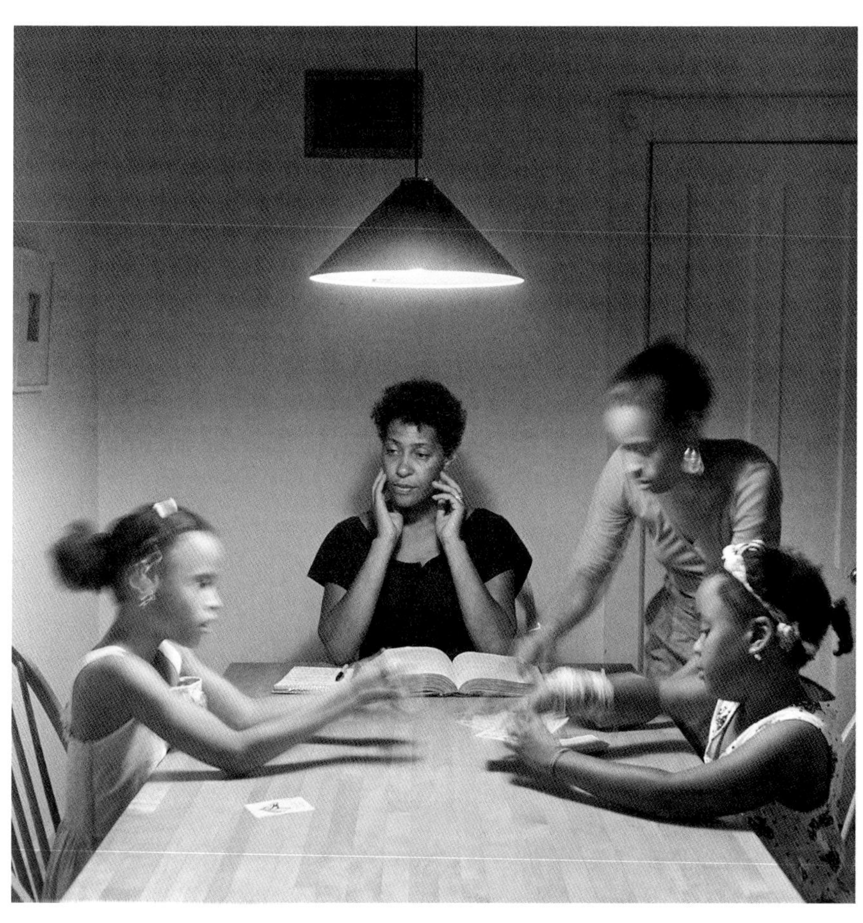

24

Carrie Mae Weems

Untitled (Woman and Daughter with Children), 1990

Gelatin silver print, 69.1 × 69.1 cm (27 3/16 × 27 3/16 in.)

Courtesy the artist and Jack Shainman Gallery,
New York, Galerie Barbara Thumm, Berlin, and
Fraenkel Gallery, San Francisco. © Carrie Mae Weems

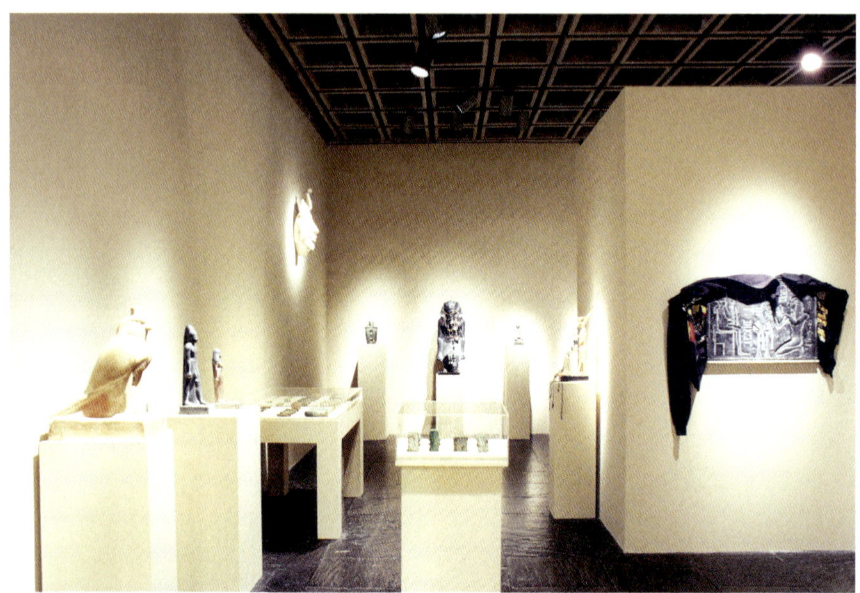

25
Installation view of the 1993 Biennial Exhibition,
Whitney Museum of American Art, New York (24
February – 20 June 1993) showing Fred Wilson's
installation *Re-Claiming Egypt* (1993) (detail)

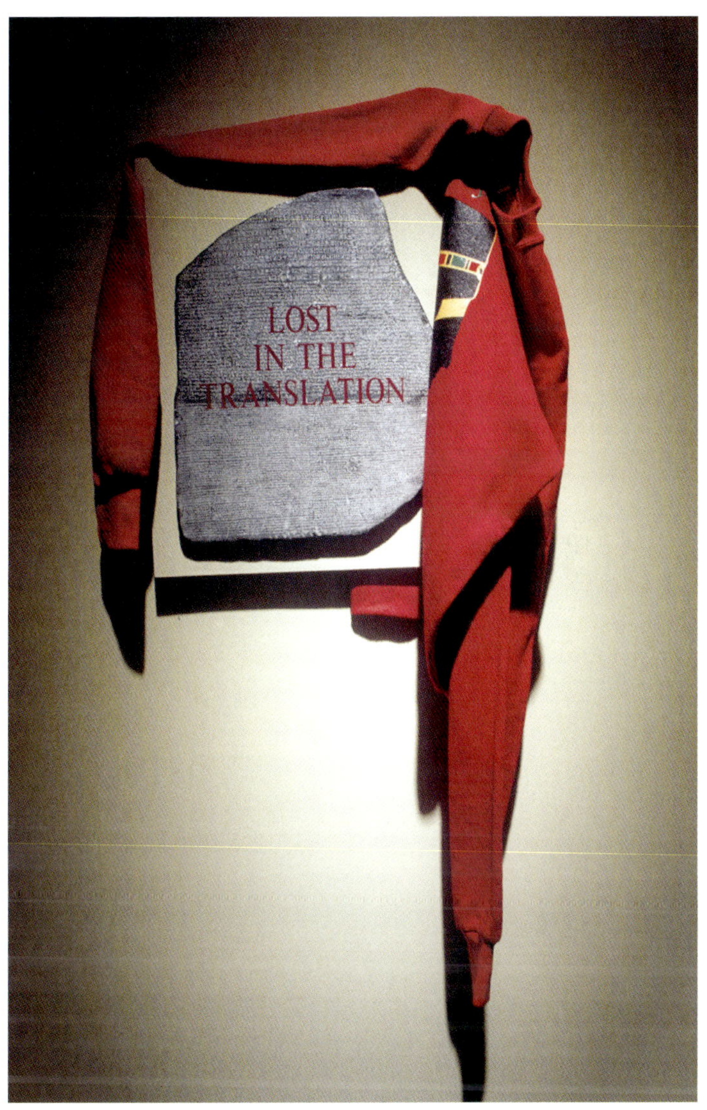

26
Installation view of the 1993 Biennial
Exhibition, Whitney Museum of American
Art, New York (24 February – 20 June 1993)
showing Fred Wilson's installation
Re-Claiming Egypt (1993) (detail)

© Fred Wilson. Photo: Geoffrey Clements. Digital image
© Whitney Museum of American Art / Licensed by Scala

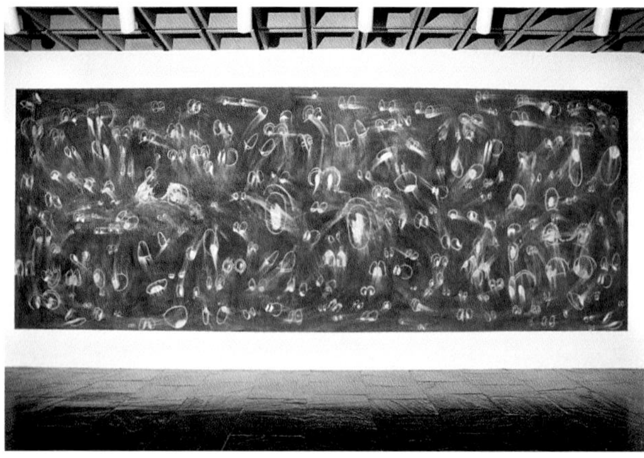

27
Installation view of the 1993 Biennial Exhibition, Whitney
Museum of American Art, New York (24 February – 20 June
1993) showing Gary Simmons's *Wall of Eyes* (1993), chalk and
chalkboard paint on wall, dimensions variable

28
Installation view of the 1993 Biennial Exhibition, Whitney
Museum of American Art, New York (24 February – 20 June 1993)
showing Lorna Simpson's *Hypothetical?* (1992)

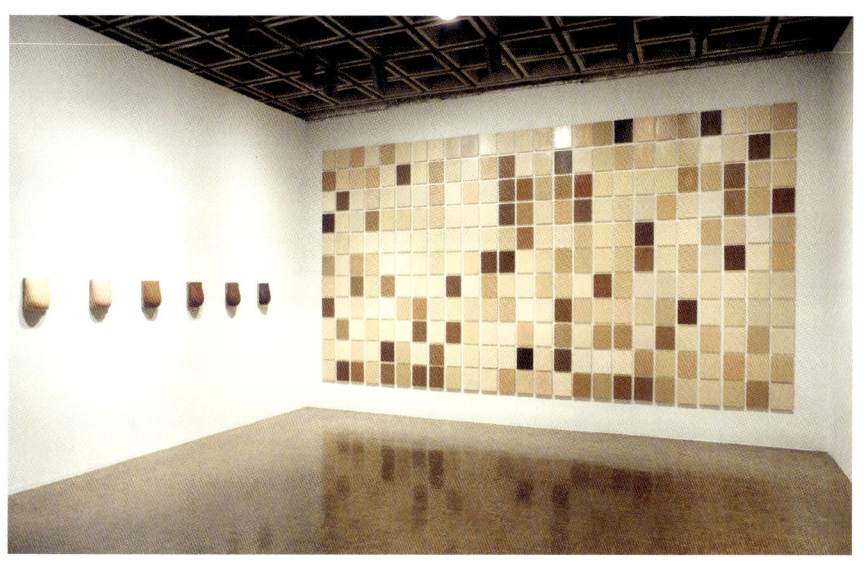

29
Installation view of the 1993 Biennial Exhibition, Whitney
Museum of American Art, New York (24 February – 20 June
1993) showing (right) Byron Kim's *Synecdoche* (1991–92),
oil and wax on wood, each panel 25.4 × 20.32 cm (10 × 8 in.),
and (left) Kim's *Belly Paintings* (1992), encaustic on linen on
panel, each panel 25.4 × 20.32 × 10.1 cm (10 × 8 × 4 in.)

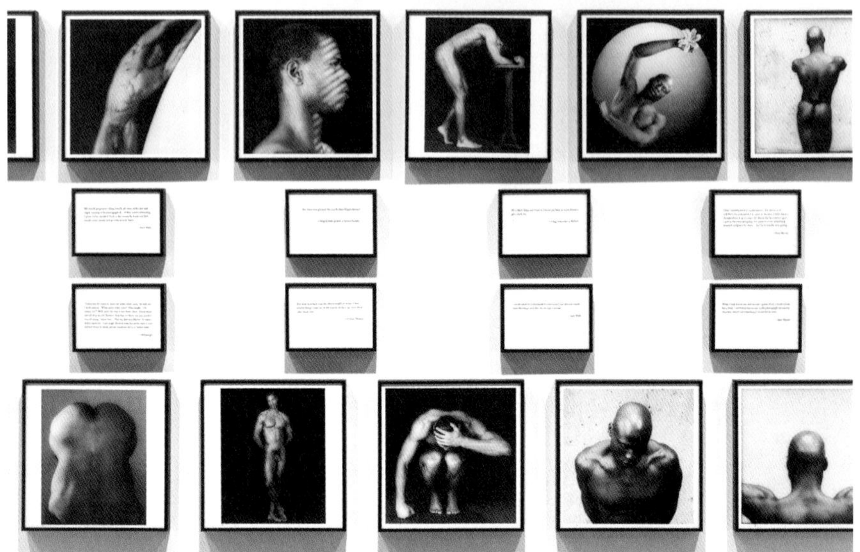

30
Glenn Ligon
Notes on the Margin of the Black Book, 1991–93 (detail)
Installation view from the exhibition *Glenn Ligon:*
AMERICA, Whitney Museum of American Art,
New York (10 March – 5 June 2011)

© Glenn Ligon. Courtesy of the artist, Hauser & Wirth, New York,
Regen Projects, Los Angeles, Thomas Dane Gallery, London, and
Galerie Chantal Crousel, Paris. Photo: Ron Amstutz

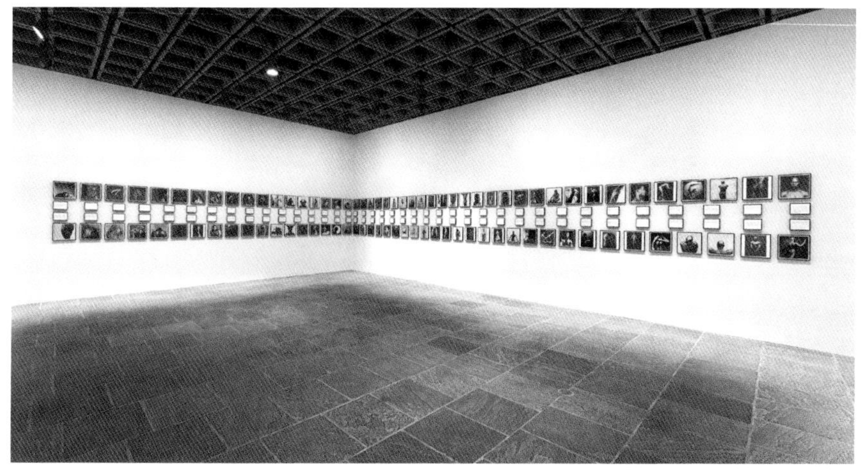

31
Glenn Ligon
Notes on the Margin of the Black Book, 1991–93
Installation view from the exhibition *Glenn Ligon:*
AMERICA, Whitney Museum of American Art,
New York (10 March – 5 June 2011)

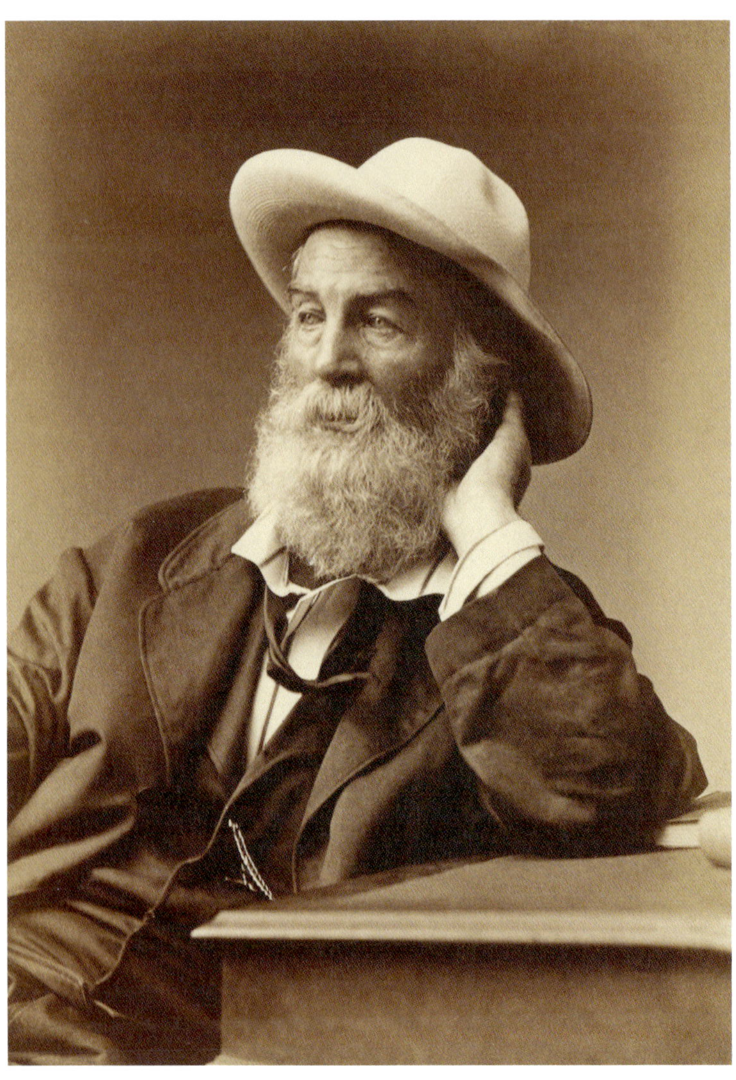

32

G. Frank E. Pearsall

Walt Whitman, September 1872

Albumen silver print, 14.1 × 10.4 cm (5 ⁹⁄₁₆ × 4 ⅛ in.)

National Portrait Gallery, Smithsonian Institution.
Gift of Mr. and Mrs. Charles Feinberg

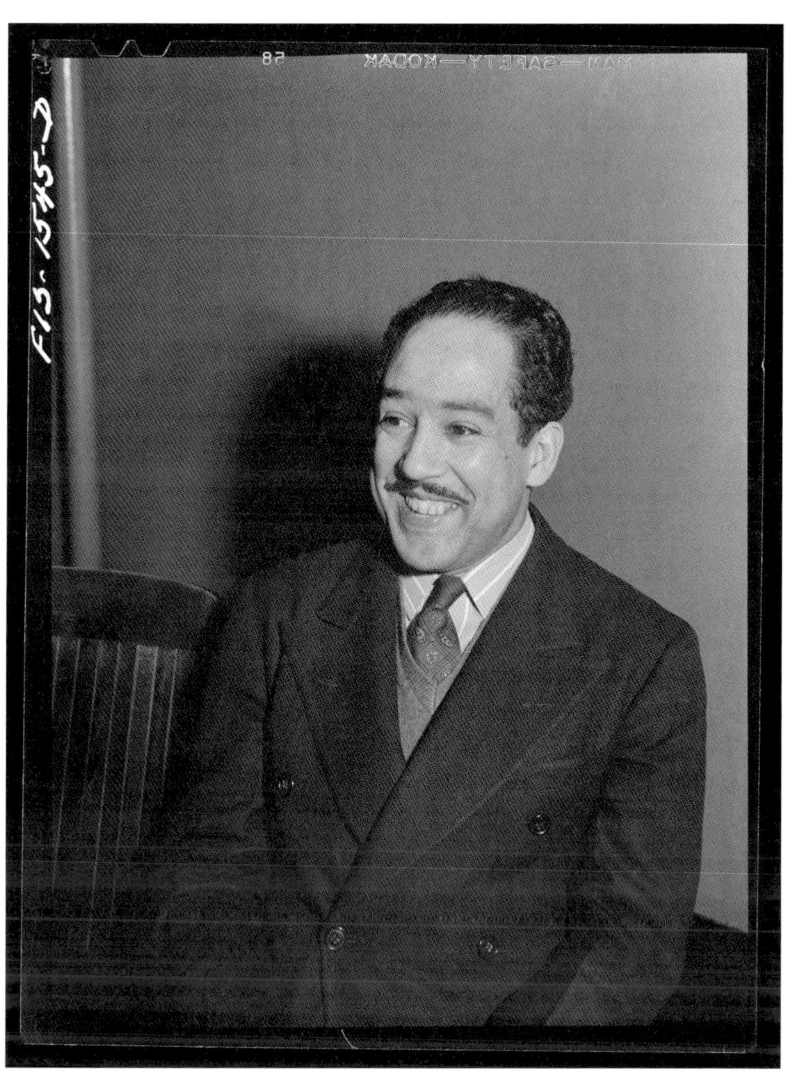

33
Jack Delano
Mr. Langston Hughes, Chicago, Illinois, 1942
Photographic-film negative

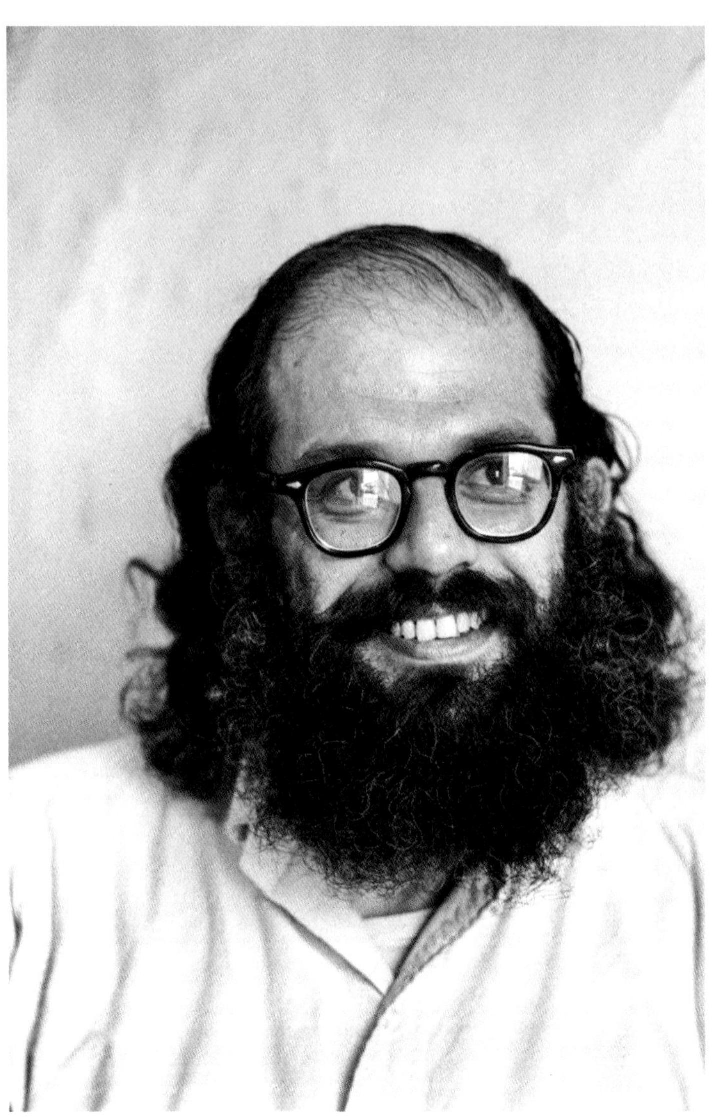

34
Allen Ginsberg at home in
New York City, 31 May 1969

Photo: David Gahr / Getty Images.
© The Estate of David Gahr

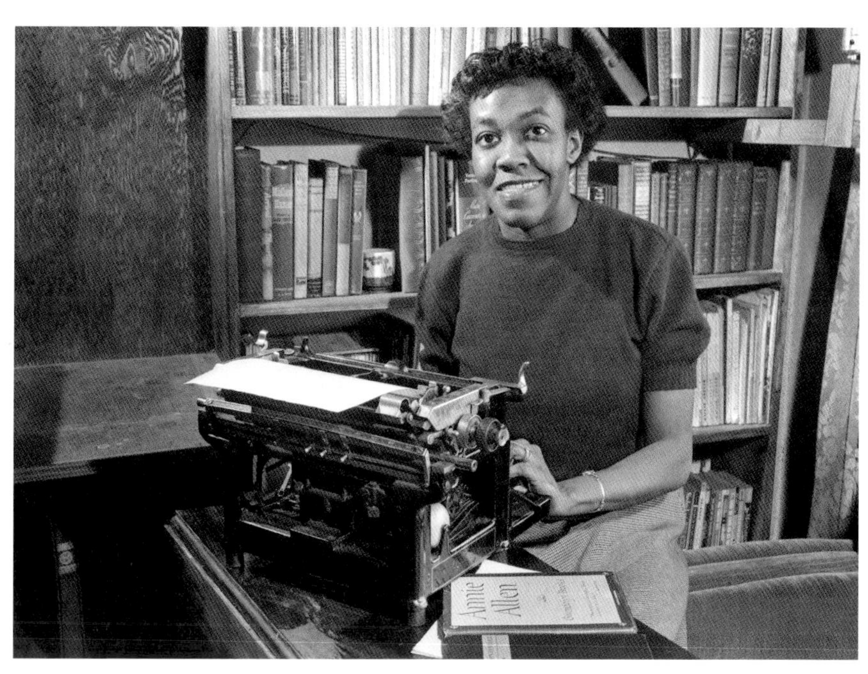

35
Gwendolyn Brooks at her typewriter
at home in Chicago, 2 May 1950

Author Biographies

Robert Storr is a curator, critic, and painter. From 1990 until 2002 he worked at The Museum of Modern Art in New York, where he was curator and then senior curator in the Department of Painting and Sculpture. His exhibitions there included *Mapping*, *DISLOCATIONS*, *Modern Art Despite Modernism*, and retrospectives of Robert Ryman, Tony Smith, Chuck Close, Gerhard Richter, Max Beckmann, and Elizabeth Murray. From 1990 to 2000 he directed MoMA's Projects program devoted to contemporary art, for which he organized small monographic shows by Art Spiegelman, Franz West, Tom Friedman, Ann Hamilton, and others. In 2002 he was named the first Rosalie Solow Professor of Modern Art at the Institute of Fine Arts, New York University where he taught through 2005. From 2006 to 2016 he served as the Stavros Niarchos Foundation Dean of the Yale University School of Art, where he continued to be a professor of painting through 2020. During that time, at the Yale University School of Art's 32 Edgewood Gallery he organized exhibitions on artists such as Francesco Clemente, Alex Katz, Jac Leirner, and Malcolm Morley, among others. He is currently Dean Emeritus and Professor Emeritus of Art at the Yale University School of Art. In 2007 he served as artistic director of the Venice Biennale, the first American to hold that position. From 2015 to 2018 he was artistic director of the video art and performance festival of the Stavros Niarchos Foundation Cultural Center (SNFCC) in Athens.

Since 1982, his essays, reviews, and columns have appeared in *Art in America*, *ARTnews*, *Art Journal*, *Artforum*, *Art Press*, *Frieze*, *Parkett*, *Corriere della Sera*, and other magazines and journals. He is the author of numerous catalogues and books—notably of *Philip Guston: A Life Spent Painting* (2020) and *Intimate Geometries: The Life and Work of Louise Bourgeois* (2016)—for the latter he received the 2017 Filaf d'or Award, as well as the 2017 Filaf Award for Best Book on Contemporary Art. He has received honorary doctorates from the School of the Art Institute of Chicago, Swarthmore College, the University of the Arts London, and the Nova Scotia College of Art and Design, among other institutions. A frequent lecturer both in the United States and abroad, he has taught painting, drawing, art history, and criticism at numerous colleges, universities, and art schools. He is the recipient of prestigious awards for his criticism and curatorial work from organizations such as the International Association of Art Critics and the Archives of American Art. In 2016 he was awarded a fellowship from the John Simon Guggenheim Memorial Foundation. Made Chevalier des Arts et des Lettres by the French Ministry of Culture in 2000, he was subsequently promoted to Officier of the same order. Storr lives and works in Brooklyn, New York, and New Haven, Connecticut.

Francesca Pietropaolo is an Italian-born art historian, curator, and critic based in Venice. Her research interests focus on international contemporary art and on postwar European and American art. She has held curatorial positions at the Walker Art Center, Minneapolis; The Museum of Modern Art, New York; the Fondazione La Biennale di Venezia, Venice; and the Fondation Louis Vuitton, Paris. During her time at MoMA, she worked on *Roth Time: A Dieter Roth Retrospective* (2004), *Plane Image: A Brice Marden Retrospective* (2006), and exhibitions drawing from the museum's collection of works on paper. She was on the curatorial team of *Greater New York 2005*, MoMA/PS, New York. At the Fondation Louis Vuitton, she was in charge of artist commissions, notably a site-specific installation by Ellsworth Kelly for the Auditorium, as well as works by Cerith Wyn Evans, Adrián Villar Rojas, and Taryn Simon, and she worked closely with artists such as Daniel Buren, Tomás Saraceno, Anthony McCall, and Lawrence Weiner. Her projects as independent curator include exhibitions such as *Wrinkles in Time* (IVAM, Valencia, 2009) and *North by New York: New Nordic Art* (American-Scandinavian Foundation, New York, 2011). At the Stavros Niarchos Foundation Cultural Center (SNFCC) in Athens, she co-curated the international video and film festival *Fireflies in the Night* (2015) and its second edition *Fireflies in the Night Take Wing* (2016), as well as the international program of performances *Only Connect!* (2017) and the video art exhibition *We Interrupt Regular Broadcasting to Bring You This Special Program!* (2018). In 2019 she co-curated the exhibition *Artists Need to Create on the Same Scale that Society Has the Capacity to Destroy: Mare Nostrum*, an official Collateral Event of the 2019 Venice Biennale held at Chiesa delle Penitenti, Venice, and she co-organized its accompanying six-month interdisciplinary public program (including poetry readings, musical performances, public conversations, film screenings, and educational workshops).

She is the editor of *Ellsworth Kelly*, first issue of "Les Cahiers de la Fondation" realized in collaboration with the artist (Fondation Louis Vuitton, Paris, 2014). She is the author of *Luisa Gardini* (De Luca Editor, Rome, 2016) and of numerous essays in publications for, among others, MoMA, the Walker Art Center, Fondation François Pinault, Kunsthaus Graz, Austria, the Estorick Collection, London, and, most recently, Académie de France à Rome. She is the editor of *Interviews on Art*, the first collection of interviews with artists conducted by Robert Storr (Heni, London, 2017) and of the two-volume collection of his *Writings on Art* (Heni, London, 2020 and 2021). As critic, she has contributed to *Flash Art International*, *ARTnews*, *Art in America*, *The Brooklyn Rail*, *Art Press*, and *Arte e Critica*. She has interviewed artists such as Rosa Barba, Y. Z. Kami, Giuseppe Penone, Doris Salcedo, and Tatiana Trouvé as well as composer Ludovico Einaudi, among others. She is editor at large at *The Brooklyn Rail*.

Acknowledgements

Firstly, our heartfelt thanks go to the artists Dawoud Bey, David Hammons, Byron Kim, Glenn Ligon, Adrian Piper, Faith Ringgold, Gary Simmons, Lorna Simpson, Carrie Mae Weems, and Fred Wilson who have agreed to participate in this project and allowed us to include reproductions of their work in this volume. We are grateful to them and their representatives.

We would also like to express our special appreciation to the following individuals for their generous cooperation in responding to our inquiries and providing images for the book (their names appear in alphabetical order): Dorian Bergen, President, ACA Galleries, New York; Samantha Cataldo, Associate Curator of Contemporary Art, Worcester Art Museum, Worcester, Massachusetts; Joseph Conder, Archivist, Hauser & Wirth, Los Angeles; Kristi L. Finefield, Reference Specialist, Prints & Photographs Division, Library of Congress; Habiba Hopson, Studio Museum in Harlem; Amy Kozlowski, Studio Assistant, Carrie Mae Weems Studio, Syracuse, New York; Lois Plehn; Tiffany Wang, Archivist, Hauser & Wirth, New York; Lucas Zenk, Director, Stephen Daiter Gallery, Chicago.

At Heni Publishing, we extend our deep thanks to Sarah McLaughlin, Production and Publications Manager, Sylvia Ugga, Book Designer, and Kirsty Watling, Editor for their dedication and careful work in the preparation of this book. We express our sincere appreciation also to Rodney Hare, CEO, Heni Group. Last but not least, to Joe Hage goes our boundless gratitude for having believed in the *Focal Points* series project from the outset and for his unwavering commitment to make it possible.

Francesca Pietropaolo and Robert Storr

Index

Focal Points

Volume 1: Bruce Nauman
Volume 2: Ad Reinhardt
Volume 3: Between a Rock and a Hard Place

Also by Robert Storr
(edited by Francesca Pietropaolo)

Interviews on Art
Writings on Art 1980–2005
Writings on Art 2006–2021